581
CAM

Camenson, Blythe

Careers for plant
lovers & other green
thumb types

$14.95

DATE			

CAREERS FOR

PLANT LOVERS
& Other Green
Thumb Types

Blythe Camenson

VGM Career Horizons
a division of *NTC Publishing Group*
Lincolnwood, Illinois USA

Dedication

To Linda Dickinson, the nicest plant lover I know.

Library of Congress Cataloging-in-Publication Data

Camenson, Blythe.
  Careers for plant lovers and other green thumb types / Blythe
Camenson.
      p.   cm.—(VGM careers for you series)
  Includes bibliographical references (p.   ).
  ISBN 0-8442-4119-9 (hc).—ISBN 0-8442-4120-2 (pbk.)
  1. Plant specialists—Vocational guidance.   I. Title.
SB50.035   1995
5818.023—dc20   95-3224
                                                                     CIP

Published by VGM Career Horizons, a division of NTC Publishing Group
4255 West Touhy Avenue
Lincolnwood (Chicago), Illinois 60646-1975, U.S.A.
© 1995 by NTC Publishing Group. All rights reserved.
No part of this book may be reproduced, stored in a retrieval system,
or transmitted in any form or by any means,
electronic, mechanical, photocopying, recording or otherwise,
without the prior permission of NTC Publishing Group.
Manufactured in the United States of America.

5 6 7 8 9 0 VP 9 8 7 6 5 4 3 2 1

Contents

About the Author

Blythe Camenson's curiosity about plants began as a child, but her first garden took a while to get off the ground—she dug up most of the plants to see how the root systems worked.

Her curiosity was more than satisfied while writing this book; she got the chance to talk to dozens of experts working in all areas of horticulture and plant science.

Blythe Camenson is a full-time writer of career books and the director of Fiction Writer's Connection, a membership organization providing support to both published and waiting-to-be-published writers. She has taught courses on freelance writing and conducts ongoing novel-writing workshops.

Camenson earned her BA in English and psychology from the University of Massachusetts in Boston and her MEd in counseling from Northeastern University, also in Boston.

She has traveled extensively and lived in the Middle East for many years. She has now settled in South Florida with her two cats and lives surrounded by semitropical greenery.

Acknowledgments

The author would like to thank the following plant lovers for providing information about their careers:

Patricia Alholm	Public Relations Manager/Marketing National Wildflower Research Center Austin, Texas
Greg Blackwell	Interiorscaper Creative Plantings Burtonsville, Maryland
Barry Brand	Grower Brand Flowers, Inc. Carpinteria, California
Anne Brennan	Student Intern Longwood Gardens Kennett Square, Pennsylvania
Kent Brinkley	Landscape Architect/Garden Historian Colonial Williamsburg Williamsburg, Virginia
Rick Darke	Curator of Plants Longwood Gardens Kennett Square, Pennsylvania
Charlene Dunn	Vice President of Marketing American Floral Services Oklahoma City, Oklahoma

Dave Foresman	Student Programs Coordinator Longwood Gardens Kennett Square, Pennsylvania
Wesley Greene	Topiary Specialist Colonial Williamsburg Williamsburg, Virginia
Robert Haehle	Garden Writer *Fort Lauderdale Sun-Sentinel* Fort Lauderdale, Florida
David Hirsch	Author and Chef Moosewood Restaurant Ithaca, New York
Loretta Hodyss	Extension Agent Cooperative Extension Service West Palm Beach, Florida
C. Way Hoyt	Arborist Tree Trimmers & Associates, Inc. Fort Lauderdale, Florida
Susan Kelley	Mapper and Labeler Arnold Arboretum Boston, Massachusetts
Richard Mattson	Professor/Horticultural Therapist Kansas State University Department of Horticulture, Forestry and Recreation Resources Manhattan, Kansas
Al Mendoza	Floral Designer/Florist/Teacher/ Commentator Keepsake Flowers and Gifts Dolton, Illinois
Sally Miller	Manager Finger Lakes Organic Growers Cooperative, Inc. Trumansburg, New York
James Moretz	Director/Photographer American Floral Art School Chicago, Illinois

Jeff Nus	Golf Course Superintendents Association of America Lawrence, Kansas
Michael O'Donnell	Nursery Owner O'Donnell Farms Coconut Creek, Florida
Pat Reese	Broker Floral International Xpress Hampshire, Illinois
Bob Scott	Director of Landscape Services Colonial Williamsburg Williamsburg, Virginia
Nancy Stevenson	Horticultural Therapist Cleveland Botanical Garden Cleveland, Ohio
Chris Strand	Outreach Horticulturist Arnold Arboretum Boston, Massachusetts
Carol Stull	Grower Finger Lakes Organic Growers Cooperative, Inc. Trumansburg, New York
Colleen Taber	Importer Gardens America, Inc. Pembroke Pines, Florida
Roy Upton	Herbalist American Herbalist Guild Soquel, California
Gordie Wilson	Superintendent, National Park Service Castillo de San Marcos National Monument St. Augustine, Florida
Rick Zenn	Education Director World Forestry Center Portland, Oregon

Surveying the Options
Jobs for Plant Lovers

W hat comes to mind when you think of paradise? A lush garden filled with thick foliage and fragrant blossoms? Nurturing sunlight, quenching rains, and a pervasive feeling of well-being?

Most people conjure up an image similar to that in one form or another. Plant lovers travel one step beyond imagination; they choose to surround themselves with paradise, living with it day to day. They know there is nothing more beautiful in the world than a flower, nothing more crucial to life than a plant.

Flowers are the symbols of health and happiness. We fill our homes with them, brighten special occasions with them, give them as tokens of love and friendship. Flowers help us to celebrate life, show our reverence or our thanks.

But their meaning is much more profound to us than mere symbols. Without plants, we would not be able to breathe. Plants absorb carbon dioxide from the air and release life-sustaining oxygen. Without plants, we would not be able to eat. Our food—vegetables, fruit, meat, grains—is all derived, directly or indirectly, from plants.

Our clothing, shelter, fuel, the medicines that keep us healthy, the paper upon which these words are printed, in fact every aspect that allows our existence to be, are all dependent upon plants and their contributions.

Plant lovers will tell you that they feel that connection between plant life and human life more strongly than other people. For a true plant lover, the opportunity to work with plants—and to earn a living doing so—is the only real definition of paradise.

What Makes a Plant Lover?

Although there probably haven't been any studies conducted to prove this, plant lovers will tell you that their love of plants is something they were born with. Not everyone grows up on a farm, or at the edge of a forest, or within walking distance of an exotic botanical garden. Yet so many city dwellers, without an inch of natural green in view, have still managed to fill their homes with foliage. Walk through any big city with tall apartment buildings and you'll still find plant-filled window boxes or balconies and terraces teeming with greenery. An aerial view would probably reveal rooftop gardens, with tubs of tomatoes or geraniums or miniature rose bushes.

This love that starts from birth generally finds its first expression during childhood. How many of us remember poking tooth picks into an avocado pit, setting it atop a glass of water, and waiting for the roots to sprout? What child hasn't nurtured the top of a carrot or planted a watermelon seed inside a tiny, windowsill pot?

Think back to your first garden—for surely, if you're reading this book, you've tended at least one garden. Do you remember planting a row of seeds; then a few days later succumbing to the temptation to sacrifice just one of them, to dig up that seed to try to understand what was happening beneath the ground? You probably remember being fascinated by the network of roots that had broken through, and marveling at the miracle of it all. The whole process of coaxing something to grow was fulfilling to you—digging in the ground, planting a seed and tending it, and watching it finally develop into something edible, or colorful or fragrant.

A love of plants *is* something we're all born with, and with the proper exposure and encouragement, which is exactly what plants need to grow, that love can be nurtured and directed into a fulfilling career.

Plant Lovers and Geography

Not every plant lover lives in—or has to live in—a tropical or semitropical location. (If that were the case, the entire globe would be tilted under the weight of plant lovers heading toward the equator to stake their claims.) Although those who do live in such areas have the longest growing seasons of all, plant lovers in other locations will tell you they manage very well.

Temperate-zone plant lovers stay up late on winter nights, arranging rows and clusters on paper, imagining the combination of colors and heights. With the first spring thaw, they're outside digging, anxious to transfer their designs to the ground.

Even plant lovers who live in the desert work with the environment they're given, studying soil conditions and what plants can thrive with a minimum of water and a maximum of heat. There are even desert-living plant lovers who seem to defy nature. With the help of extra soil and water, they establish greenery where greenery couldn't possibly grow.

With today's modern technology, plants can grow anywhere. Hothouses and experimental bubble gardens abound, as do the people who plan and tend them.

Do You Have What It Takes?

Plant lovers are nurturers and givers. To be a gardener, for example, takes commitment and the ability to assume responsibility. Just as every mother in the animal kingdom tends her young, so must plant lovers care for their charges. You're keeping something alive, after all.

Plant lovers aren't afraid to get their hands dirty. In fact, they relish the feel of good, rich soil.

Plant lovers also have a strong sense of design; they can take a myriad of simple materials—flowers, moss, leaves, grasses, stone, wood, bailing wire, copper tubing, spray paint—and create remarkable and breathtaking arrangements, or they can look at a bare plot of ground and see the endless possibilities for as many different garden styles.

Here are some other qualities that plant lovers possess. How many apply to you?

A curious nature and a sense of adventure

Good business sense

Organizational skills

A thirst for knowledge

An understanding of the environment

Knowledge of pests and pesticides

Writing and communication skills

An eagerness to work hard

A willingness to earn a meager to average salary

Not all of these qualities are necessary for fulfillment in every aspect of horticulture work, but you should have been able to check off a good number of them. The most successful people have a combination of on-the-job experience, education, and knowledge of every aspect of the related horticulture industries.

What Does the Terminology Mean?

Throughout this book you will run across several terms used to describe designated fields of interest or career categories. Sometimes the terms may be used interchangeably. Here are some simple definitions to guide you.

Horticulture is the broadest category. It covers all commercial and scientific enterprises involving flowers, vegetables, fruits, grass, turf management, groundskeeping, and forestry. Horticulturists work in every aspect of the plant field, from cultivation, wholesaling, and retailing to design, management, and scientific study.

Floriculture is a specific area of horticulture. The word is derived from the Latin and literally means "to cultivate flowers." But it involves much more than that. Floriculture is both an art and a science; it is the field of growing, marketing, and designing with flowers and plants.

Ornamental horticulture is another specific category of the general term horticulture. Ornamental means decorative and refers to decorative plants. It covers landscaping and interiorscaping, and **amenity horticulture**—anything that makes the environment more beautiful.

Floral design is the most specific category within ornamental horticulture. It encompasses the arranging, selling, and marketing and merchandising of fresh flowers and plants for the home, hospital, or special occasion.

Career Options in Horticulture

Plant lovers find careers in a variety of traditional and innovative areas. They work with decorative plants and flowers as florists or floral designers. They grow plants for food or for their aesthetic value. They tend and nurture plants as groundskeepers, golf course workers, or plant sitters. They beautify our surroundings as landscape designers or landscape architects. They work in our homes, designing the "interiorscaping." They study, arrange, sort, identify, and exhibit plants. They photograph plants and write about them, and educate others about their value.

What follows is an overview of general categories. You can learn more about each career in the chapters ahead.

Decorative Flowers and Plants

Florists, ornamental horticulturists, floral designers, floriculturists (flower growers), wholesalers, and retailers all work with decorative plants and flowers. They own and operate or work in florist shops and nurseries. They cultivate bonsai or design topiary displays. They brighten weddings and birthdays and other special occasions or use flowers and plants to craft works of art or items with specific useful functions.

There are also several new career categories popping up in the floricultural industry including horticultural therapy, brokering, and commentating.

Successful plant lovers working in floriculture and ornamental horticulture generally have business skills as well as a refined sense of design.

Caring for Plants

Skilled plant lovers find careers taking care of other people's plants. They work as foresters or professional pathologists, plant doctors, or tree surgeons, identifying problems and working to cure them. Some operate plant rental services to help beautify private homes or office buildings. As part of the service, they visit the locations where they have leased their plants and water and feed them, replacing them if the sites do not offer the best conditions.

Other enterprising plant lovers seek out vacation-planning customers and provide plant sitting services. These care givers are self-employed or work for nurseries or other plant outlets.

Botanical Gardens and Arboreta

Botanical gardens and arboreta offer a range of jobs for plant lovers. This setting utilizes guides and educators, identifiers, curators, mappers and labelers, exhibitors, propagators, and scientists. Botanical gardens and arboreta are located throughout the country.

Landscaping

Landscape architects and landscape designers are accomplished professionals who work with clients to beautify and protect our surroundings. They study space allocations and environmental conditions, choosing the best plants and layout for the location. They find jobs through the government and private sectors or through self-employment.

Groundskeeping

Groundskeepers love the outdoors and care for parks, golf courses, cemeteries, private homes, and public property. They work for city, state, or federal government agencies or for private enterprises. Many are self-employed.

The Study of Plants

Scientists study all aspects of plant life such as growing conditions, plant diseases, energy conservation, and production research. They work in universities or for botanical gardens and nurseries. They make contributions to many fields such as agriculture or medicine. They even work underwater, studying marine life and other aspects of oceanography.

Writing about Plants and Photographing Them

Plant lovers with a flair for the written word create instructional "how-to" gardening books or write articles and columns for magazines and newspapers. Many are self-employed, working as freelancers; others work for a variety of regional and/or national publications. Many photographers specialize in capturing images of plants and flowers on film. They publish their work in books or in magazines and newspapers. They chronicle events at floral design competitions or create the colorful photographs and catalogs florists use to sell their arrangements.

Food and Medicinal Plants

Plant lovers find satisfying careers working with food or medicinal plants. They work in agriculture as farmers, farm advisors, specialty breeders, wholesalers, and retailers.

If their interests tend toward the medicinal value of plants, they find careers as herbologists, botanical pharmacologists, or in homeopathic medicine.

Educators

Educators work in schools and universities, botanical gardens and arboreta, or for government agencies such as the Cooperative Extension Service. They teach future plant scientists, professional groundskeepers, or amateur gardeners. They share their knowledge and the results of plant research to help all plant-related professionals.

The Job Outlook

The job outlook for plant lovers is very good. The Society of American Florists asserts the following: "Presently, the number of graduates from two- and four-year colleges and technical programs is not sufficient to meet the increasing needs of the industry." This situation covers almost all horticultural-related fields, from floral design to cultivators and retailers.

The more education and on-the-job training and experience you have, and the more individualized skills you have picked up along the way, the better your job prospects.

The Training You'll Need

The training required for the various fields in horticulture vary greatly. Some positions are entry level, requiring no more than a high school education or the ability to engage in heavy manual labor. Others require specific skills and from two to four years of college or a technical program. Still others require postgraduate study at the master's or doctoral level.

Resources are listed throughout each chapter to tell you about job possibilities and avenues for education and/or on-the-job training.

CHAPTER TWO

Careers in Floriculture
Working with Decorative Flowers and Plants

T he art and science of floriculture can be viewed as a series of stages. First the flowers must be grown and tended; then made available to retailers. Before the customer can have an order filled, the flowers must be tended to again, made into creative arrangements, or placed in strategic locations within the home or office.

Plant lovers can find a variety of careers working in the various stages of floriculture. The options include growing, importing, wholesaling and brokering, retailing, designing, interiorscaping, and commentating. These job titles and others are covered in this chapter.

Growing Plants

A grower starts the beginning of the process and in many ways performs the most crucial function in the chain. Without the expertise and care of an experienced grower, there would be no flowers to market to the general public.

The grower deals with the basics; she plants bulbs or seeds in the ground and raises them to sell as cut flowers. Her customers are wholesalers, brokers, retailer florists, and nursery owners.

Although many of the cut flowers available for sale in the United States are grown in other countries (see "Importers" later in this chapter), U.S. growers can still flourish here on native soil.

As Barry Brand, a grower based in Carpinteria, California explains it, "Most of the flowers grown in other countries are roses and carnations and chrysanthemums. But we don't grow those. I looked for different niches in the marketplace and I grow flowers that are difficult to grow. As long as you do it well, you can be successful."

Barry owns three different farms with more than 100 acres. Some of his land supports greenhouses and shadehouses (structures that protect the flowers from the sun). The largest amount of acreage is devoted to field flowers.

He grows a variety of crops including lilies, freesias, tulips, gerbera, delphinium, larkspur, snapdragons, sunflowers, and alstroemeria. Last year he reports that business was booming—$5 million dollar's worth, in fact. Each year millions and millions of stems (the way flowers are counted) go from Barry's farms to market.

Cut-Flower Growing Job Titles

Running a big operation like Barry's requires a healthy number of workers. Barry has about 74 employees. The job titles found in cut-flower growing include the following:

Field workers As their job title implies, field workers are found in the field taking care of the different crops. They plant and weed and pick the flowers when they are ready for market.

Foremen Each crop has its own foreman who oversees the field workers. The foreman is responsible for all the daily care the flowers need.

Production managers Production managers report back to the head grower or owner and keep track of all the different crops. They are responsible for overall production including taking care of fertilizing and pesticide spraying schedules.

Graders The graders sort through the flowers, dividing them into bunches in three different groups based on their quality.

Sales staff The salespeople contact wholesalers and retailers across the country, letting them know what crops are available for sale.

Data entry and office workers The office staff take care of computerizing sales information and all the other administrative tasks involved with running a cut-flower farm.

Warehouse staff The warehouse staff take care of the flowers when they come in from the field and get them ready to go out to market. They supervise the coolers and are responsible for packing the flowers in boxes for shipping.

How Barry Brand Got His Start

Barry grew up in Holland where he completed a three-year course in floriculture. "My father was a grower in Holland and the original plan was for me to become a partner with him, but I wanted to see the United States before I did that. After I visited here, I decided to stay."

That was in 1985. During his first year here Barry worked for different nurseries, learning the ropes. Then his brother and father left Holland to join him in California. Barry and his brother started a small family nursery growing snapdragons, leasing the property rather than buying it. Every month their operation grew and after one year their father joined them in partnership. By 1989 they had expanded so much that they split the nursery into two different operations and Barry formed a new business partnership with his wife, who now works with him at their three California farms.

He now owns most of the land outright. Barry sums it up: "We started with nothing, and now we're doing pretty well."

The secret to his success? "I think we grow the right crops and we put a lot of time into it. We also have the belief that we can do it. I always knew that I was going to be a flower grower. You don't take 'no' for an answer—you just have to believe in yourself."

Having a great love for what you do is also important. "I've always liked working with nature. Every day is different, a challenge. It's never boring."

WHAT IT TAKES Barry Brand's advice is for any potential grower to go to school. "Learn as much as you can about plants, but also about business. Studying business in school was a big help to me. My wife, Wilja, who is also my partner, has a strong business background, too. This is probably why we're so successful.

"Also, before I started my own, I worked for a lot of other nurseries. You learn from how other people run their businesses. Even if you grew up on a farm, you should work for other people first, in any position you can, before you start out on your own. I started as a field worker, then worked my way up to manager. You can't be afraid to work."

Selling Plants

Importer

Most of the flowers that you'll order from a florist shop have not been grown domestically. Although some originate in Europe, in particular in Holland, most are imported to the U.S. from Central and South America. In general, costs are lower there, land is less expensive, and the climatic conditions are more favorable, saving the expense of heating greenhouses.

Importers coordinate all the various steps involved with bringing in flowers from growers or suppliers in other countries. They are responsible for the masses of paperwork necessary before the flowers can be shipped to the various wholesalers, brokers, or retail outlets. Some of the documentation is for plant inspections, plant quarantines, and Customs.

Colleen Taber, Importer

Colleen Taber has been in the cut-flower import business for more than twenty years and in the spring of 1994 she became the sole owner of her company, Gardens America. Most importers are based in southern Florida and Colleen's sales office is in Pembroke Pines, near Miami. She also has a warehouse on a runway of Miami International Airport so flowers can go directly from the plane to the cooler.

Although most importers bring in flowers from a variety of different growers, Colleen works with only one supplier, Gardens of the Andes, which is based in Bogota, Columbia. "I find if I give all of my attention to the one grower, that's what the grower gives back to me," Colleen explains. "Because of the relationship with the grower, I can tell them a year in advance what I need them to grow for me, what color varieties I need each week, what I need for a holiday, and I know that their only concern is me. We work that well together that I can send out promotional material to the customer and they'll know that on week three, for example, they'll have pom poms and alstroemeria in the boxes; on week 22, lilies, fujis, and carnations. There's never a guess."

Although Colleen works with only one grower, she in turn sells to more than 300 customers in the United States. "I'm unique in the way I work," Colleen says. "I'm the only importer who sells strictly on a standing-order basis. That means that I call customers, or customers call me and say they would like to be a customer of Gardens America. I process their credit application and then I take their order—which is for the same amount every week of the year. So the flowers come in here already sold. Other importers bring in the product and store it in the cooler while they're trying to sell it."

COLLEEN'S BACKGROUND   Colleen started in the business working for her parents, who were the original owners of Gardens America, and learned everything from the ground up. Her advice: "For everything you learn, you can learn two things by your mistakes. So I made sure I made plenty of mistakes. Not by choice, really, just by sheer lack of skill. But what I found is that with the world so competitive, it's much better to have some kind of formal training. We employ three full-time sales people who sell to 300 customers and do more than $21 million in sales each year. But my sales staff never really had any formal training. Recently, we all enrolled in a Dale Carnegie sales course and we have seen a big difference."

Training for Importers

If you want to work as an importer, Colleen's suggestion is to try to get a job with an importer, doing whatever you can get hired to do. "You can never see a picture as clearly from the top as from the bottom," she says.

Alternatively, Colleen recommends finding work with a broker who handles all the paperwork that goes to Customs. "Or, get a job with U.S. Customs," Colleen suggests. "Then you can see what happens and what all the pitfalls are. You have to be very careful, especially when you're dealing with South America where there are such strong drug implications. It's a real hardship for legitimate growers who have to go to extremes to make sure nothing gets into the boxes of flowers except flowers. And on this end, every single package is x-rayed and filmed. They even identify the packer, they initial each box. The precautions are very detailed."

Positions with an Importer

The number of staff varies with the size of each business. Colleen employs one assistant, three salespeople, one bookkeeper, one receptionist, one billing clerk, one statistician (who takes care of tracking all the sales figures), and four packers and shippers who handle all operations at her warehouse.

Salaries with an Importer

Salaries also vary from importer to importer. In general, however, sales people can make the best living. Although some importers pay their staff on a commission (1.5 to 2.5 percent of collected sales) or commission-plus-salary basis, Colleen reports that members of her sales staff working with the standing order accounts earn a set salary of approximately $52,000 per year.

And while warehouse staff who basically move boxes around might earn just above minimum wage for other importers, at Gardens America they earn between $20,000 and $25,000 a year. "I do as well as I do with few people," Colleen explains, "because I pay them well and treat them well, and then they work better."

Brokers and Wholesalers

Brokers and wholesalers perform similar functions. They purchase stock directly from growers or importers and supply florists with fresh flowers, decorative plants, and other related items. However, how they work with the florists differs a great deal.

Based on the estimated need of their regular customers, wholesalers buy a certain quantity of flowers each week at a price determined by the growers or importers. This could be, for example, 1,000 boxes of fresh carnations (with 600 carnations to a box), 500 cases of pom poms, and 50 dozen roses. At the beginning of the week, when the florists' coolers need replenishing and the wholesalers' stock is fresh, the wholesalers add in their expenses and set a profit to the price given to the florists. As the week goes by and the flowers are no longer in peak condition, the wholesaler will adjust the price downward, according to what the market can bear. The wholesalers' earning power can see a great deal of fluctuation.

Wholesalers receive their flowers from their suppliers, and store them, usually in a refrigerated warehouse, provide them with any care and conditioning they need, and then deliver them to the florists. The florists are usually located within an easy delivery distance from the wholesaler, most likely within a fifty-mile radius.

In addition to standing orders, wholesalers supply florists with special orders. They can send over one rare bird of paradise or a half dozen orchids for a bride's bouquet.

Brokers go directly to the grower or importer and get a price for a particular item. That price is set for the day and will not change. After adding on a profit margin to the price, the broker then, usually over the telephone, sells the stock to the florists. Only after she has actually sold the flowers will the broker go back to the grower and plant down her money, so to speak.

This procedure of selling stock at a guaranteed price eliminates all risk for the broker. In addition, she is not responsible for warehousing and taking care of plants. She doesn't even have to get involved in shipping; the grower or importer can send the purchase overnight directly to the florist, who can be located anywhere in the country.

On the surface, considering the benefits to the broker, it is surprising that there are any wholesalers in business. They have all the financial risk and most of the responsibility of keeping the flowers in good condition. A broker needs only a telephone and a good sales pitch.

However, most retail florist shops prefer to work with local wholesalers. The florist can drop in, see what's in stock, and pick out a few of this and a few of that. Wholesalers will handle special orders or spur-of-the moment deliveries. Wholesalers will also give the florist a call every morning and ask what she needs. The order is then placed on the truck and is delivered by the afternoon. Brokers are not equipped to do this. The customers brokers deal with are usually large retail outlets that handle a large volume of business. They place orders on a weekly, or twice weekly, as opposed to a daily basis. Many florists work with both brokers and wholesalers. They get their day-to-day orders through the wholesaler and go to brokers to supplement that with the larger orders they know in advance they're regularly going to need. For example, if a florist knows he'll regularly sell 100 carnations a week, he'll place that order through a broker. The other orders such as for weddings or funerals will go to the wholesaler.

A Pioneer in the Brokering Business

Pat Reese started as a broker 15 years ago. "I'd like to think, though I can't prove this, that I was, if not the first, then at least the second, broker in cut flowers. When I started there really was no one else doing this. It was all by the traditional wholesaling method. Now, of course, there are quite a few brokers. And what has happened is that many of the growers have seen what a brokering business can do and they have formed their own brokerage companies."

Pat Reese started out working with a floral publishing company as an advertising manager. He stayed with them for nine years; then went on to the flower-by-wire service business as a field representative with Teleflora. (You'll find more information about careers with wire services later in this chapter under "Selling.") When he left Teleflora 15 years ago to become a broker, he was Vice President of Sales in California.

"After having spent almost 20 years of my adult life being in and around florist shops, I kept seeing a need for a more efficient system. I was running into disgruntled florists all the time who were upset with their local wholesalers for a hundred different reasons. At the same time the FAX machine was just starting to make its way in and transportation was something I'd always been interested in, and it became a desire to find a different way.

I wanted to build a better mousetrap. And I did. I took my idea to three former presidents of Teleflora and each one of them became a full partner in my company, which is called "Floral International Xpress" or FIX. I was the operating officer and they were investors."

Since then, Pat has bought out his investors and is now sole proprietor.

What You'll Need to Become a Wholesaler or Broker

Pat Reese suggests that the first thing you should do if you're interested in this kind of career is to make sure you know the flower industry. When he plunged in, he already knew thousands of florists on a first-name basis and had a ready-made list of customers.

You also have to have a good sales background, Pat advises, and, for brokering, you need telemarketing skills. Most, if not all, of your selling will be done over the telephone. You need to know about distribution and also have a strong financial background.

A source of start-up capital is also necessary, for both brokering and wholesaling, although the amount is usually smaller for the new broker. Brokers don't have overhead to worry about, or warehouses or refrigeration or insurance and employees and delivery. They can work anywhere they can install a telephone.

But for both professions, until you've established yourself with the growers and importers, you'll have to pay up front for the goods you purchase. There's always a gap of time before you get paid by the florists and you have to be able to cover yourself during that period.

Florists

Florists either own and operate their own shops or work in a shop for someone else. There are three kinds of flower shops: cash and carry stores, decorator shops, and service shops.

Cash and carry stores, or merchandising stores as they are also known, sell bunches of prewrapped flowers. Generally, customers cannot order special arrangements through cash and carry shops; their selections are limited to what is immediately available and on hand. Cash and carry shops are found in the neighborhood supermarket's flower section, at farmers' markets, or at impromptu "shops" set up in buckets alongside the road.

Decorator shops, which are few and far between, operate as specialists, custom-making arrangements for important occasions such as weddings or balls. They generally do not cater to walk-in customers.

The largest percentage of florists are service florists, meaning they offer a service in addition to a product. They design and custom-make and deliver their merchandise.

The jobs available in florist shops include owner, manager, salesperson, floral designer, delivery personnel, interiorscaping, and maintenance personnel.

Location, Location, Location

As with any business that hopes to garner off-the-street customers, location is always the first consideration. Because flowers are considered to be more a luxury item than a necessity (although fervent plant lovers would surely argue for the latter definition), most successful florist shops are found in suburban town centers as opposed to downtown, inner city locations. Florist shops also can do well in shopping malls.

The Skills You'll Need

To be a successful florist, a love of plants, although crucial, is not enough. Florists must have training in every aspect of the industry, including strong business skills. The best preparation is gaining a combination of on-the-job experience and education.

Trainees can gain experience working part-time for retail and wholesale florists, for greenhouses and nurseries, or for cut-flower growers. With this kind of exposure, potential florists can learn about packing and unpacking, processing, shipping, propagation, cutting, seed sowing, bulb planting and potting, the basics of floral design, and pickup, delivery, and sales work.

While in school, students should take courses in biological sciences, math, communications, computer science, and general business, including retail store management.

Some academic and vocational institutions offer two- and four-year programs geared directly to floriculture and horticulture. Many also provide students with the opportunity for training while in school through cooperative education programs. Coop programs place students in related business settings and, after the first year of academics, alternate semesters with work and study.

The Society of American Florists has prepared a list of colleges, universities, and postsecondary schools offering two- and four-year degree programs and technical and certificate-awarding programs. The courses cover general horticulture, ornamental horticulture, floriculture, and floral design. The Society's address can be found at the end of this chapter.

The Downsides of the Job

Florists work long hours and as Al Mendoza, proprietor of Keepsake Flowers and Gifts in Dolton, Illinois, says, "When most people are out enjoying the various parties, you're working at them. During holiday times, most people are having fun, enjoying the festivities, but again, it's the busiest time of the year for florists. In the floral world you don't get weekends and holidays off. I can't remember the last time my family and I could share a decent holiday together. Christmas, Easter. You're working like crazy the week before; then you're so exhausted, you can't enjoy yourself." (Al Mendoza talks more about his work later in this chapter under "Floral Designing.")

The Finances

To start a florist shop these days an initial investment of about $50,000 would be required. And in today's economy, Al says, you can expect to work eight to ten years before realizing a profit.

"It's a risk when you're dealing with perishables. A person could lose a lot if they don't know how to order. If they order too much they can lose, or if they don't order enough they can lose. A typical example would be Valentine's Day. If you order too many roses, if you buy a thousand too many, you can lose thousands of dollars. But it's hard to learn how to get the ordering right. That's why it's so important to work for other florists before venturing out on your own. You need the experience."

Retail Nurseries

Although some florists might occasionally grow their own plants to sell, most of the time they purchase their products from wholesalers or brokers. Nurseries, on the other hand, generally grow on site most of the products they sell to the public.

O'Donnell Farms

Michael O'Donnell is proprietor of O'Donnell Farms, a wholesale and retail nursery and garden center in Coconut Creek, Florida. "Most of the things we sell we grow ourselves," Michael explains, "and there are certain things we buy. Nobody in this business raises everything. There are at least 1,800,000 species of plants. We grow more than 700 different types of items here. But we're a bit unusual in that respect. Most nurseries grow only a dozen or so items."

O'Donnell Farms raises shade trees, a large selection of palms, bushes, ground covers, orchid plants, and house plants. Michael O'Donnell started out as a hobbyist and was actively involved in the American Orchid Society. In addition, he comes to the nursery field with many years of experience in the business world. "I think it's very helpful to have a business background coupled with horticultural knowledge. You have to be familiar with production management, buying, selling, pricing, maintenance, care. This is like our own little world here. We have our own electrical and plumbing systems, we propagate plants from seed and stem cuttings and meristem tissue culture. We try to be self-sufficient."

Positions in a Nursery

Nurseries employ a wide range of personnel. O'Donnell Farms has a landscape designer (see Chapter Three for more information on that career), a landscape supervisor who oversees the outside jobs, a nursery supervisor who oversees the propagation of the plant material and directly manages the employees under him, field workers who take care of growing all the plants, a maintenance foreman who keeps a large fleet of trucks, front loaders, and cranes in working operation, office staff (a secretary and bookkeeper), and a sales staff.

Training for Nursery Work

Sales staff, field workers, and supervisors all must be knowledgeable about all aspects of both indoor and outdoor gardening, from soil conditions to fertilizers and pesticides. They have to be familiar with all the different plants: where they come from, what they're called, how to grow them, how to take care of them.

Some education in horticulture is essential, as is hands-on training and on-the-job experience.

Salaries for Nursery Workers

Salaries can range from $5.50 to $10 an hour to $25,000 to $60,000 a year, depending on the position you land. Sales staff working on commissions and landscape designers and supervisors generally make the most money. A field worker caring for orchids might start out at a lower salary, but it would be possible to work her way up the ladder into management.

But if the salaries don't quite measure up, most dedicated plant lovers don't seem to mind. As Michael O'Donnell puts it, the attraction is "to work with living material, to watch something grow. It's like a call of nature. Some people are called to the sea, some people are called to the plant world. I've done everything I've wanted to do with my life—I wanted to be the president of a big company and I've done that, and now I'm doing exactly what I want to do."

Wire Services

It's Valentine's Day and a young man working in Seattle telephones or visits a local florist. He chooses a traditional dozen red roses (long stems) and has them sent to his fiancée who is attending school in Boston, Massachusetts. He pays by credit card over the phone, or by credit card, check, or cash in person. The Seattle florist contacts a Boston shop and in no time, the young woman receives her Valentine's gift.

The Seattle florist took the order, arranged for the flowers, and collected the money. The Boston florist provided the flowers and had them delivered. But how does that shop receive payment?

Through the wire services. There are six major wire services in the country (FTD, Teleflora, AFS, Florafax, Carik, and Redbook) and they act as clearinghouses for the financial transactions between participating florists around the country.

Charlene Dunn, Vice President of Marketing at AFS (American Floral Services), the largest of the wire services, explains, "When a florist sends an order to another state, for example, the florist on the sending side has the money, the florist on the receiving end has done most of the work. What we do is take the money from one and we give it to the other—assuring that payment is made to that person."

Jobs with a Wire Service

Wire services offer a range of positions—AFS, for example, employs approximately 160 people—falling into the following job titles: executive officers, financial officers, credit and statement clerks, human resource workers (personnel), operations workers, directory service workers (the people who publish the directories of participating florists), customer services, international relay services, field staff, and educators.

Field staff are mainly marketing counselors whose job is to go from shop to shop offering help. They must have a sales background and knowledge of the floral industry. "Partly what they do," Charlene explains, "is make sure that florists have what they need as far as the services we offer. In addition to the financial end of things, AFS is involved in other related activities. We have design and management training, educational publications, and computer software to improve the efficiency, profitability, and professionalism of AFS florists. We also help with marketing and provide point-of-purchase products such as window posters and banners advertising various holiday arrangements."

Wire services employ field staff all over the country. When an opening comes up, they advertise it in the local newspaper in the area where they need to hire someone. The advertisements would usually be found under "Sales."

"We also employ a large number of educators to help with professional floral development," says Charlene. "Thousands of florists from around the world have attended our education center. We offer programs in floral design, commentating, management, and computer skills. We also go out into the field and train florists across the country through our seminars. Some of the topics we cover are the care and handling of flowers and financial management techniques. We also conduct classes in the Pacific rim teaching Western-style floral design."

Educators working with AFS are all experienced professionals in their various fields—from successful florists and floral designers to computer and financial experts.

Designing

Floral Designers

"Say It with Flowers" was a campaign slogan the Society of American Florists coined and publicized in a million-dollar advertising campaign begun in 1924. Since that time millions of consumers have been doing just that—saying it with flowers—on Mother's Day and Valentine's Day, at senior proms and on graduation day, at weddings and churches, at hospitals and funerals, at dinner parties and elegant society balls. But without florists, and more specifically, floral designers, we wouldn't have much to say it with.

Commercial floral designers brighten almost every occasion, coordinating colors, shaping moods, creating atmosphere and beauty. They find work in commercial or specialty florist shops, as florist shop owners/designers, or as straight designers. A few find unusual and rewarding job settings such as consulting for the annual Rose Bowl Parade or commentating and judging at high level competitions or garden and flower shows.

They custom-make arrangements to the specific needs of the client, or fabricate their own creations using a few of the following popular design styles:

In a **pillowing** design, the arrangement resembles fleecy clouds. The flowers are placed up and down and are packed close together with some depth to them.

Pavé, meaning pavement, is the opposite of the pillowing design. With pavé, everything is exactly the same size and very flat.

In a **parallel** design the flowers are like soldiers standing at attention. The word *parallel* is from the Greek meaning "side by side." The stems are straight up and down and parallel to each other. The arrangement can be vertical, horizontal, or diagonal.

New Convention has an architectural look. There are lines straight up and lines at a 90-degree angle straight out. There are no 45-degree angles—in other words, nothing is leaning. This arrangement can resemble the skyline of a city seen on the horizon.

The Romantic Look is from the Victorian era, featuring little handheld poseys, or Tussey Musseys as they are called.

Training for Floral Designers

In addition to owning Keepsake Flowers, Al Mendoza is also assistant director at the American Art Floral School. "I can take someone off the street and teach them design," Al says. "It's very mechanical. You establish your height, your width, your depth. The art part is where the talent comes in."

Many floral designers get their training working in a florist shop, learning as they go. They also attend seminars and workshops and take courses at floral design schools. The American Floral Art School, in business for over 50 years, is one of the best known in the world. It offers an intensive three-week course, after which Al Mendoza says students will graduate as competent designers with a good understanding of the basics. "A three-week course," Al explains, "is enough to help a student get his foot in the door at a flower shop. But really, three weeks is not enough. The rest of the training comes from on-the-job experience. But it's a Catch-22 situation. It's difficult to get that first job without some sort of training. Our program helps to open the door."

There are no prerequisites to attend the school; a high school diploma or a college degree are not necessary to enter the field of floral design—although some academic preparation is recommended.

Al says, "I always tell any student who is coming to our school and planning on opening up a flower shop that it's great to know floral design, but it's more important to have a business degree than a floral degree. More businesses fail because they think of it as an art business rather than an actual commercial business. If someone wants to get their training through college, they should major in business with a minor in floral design."

During the three-week program at the American Floral Art School students study art and mechanics. "The art is what you see in a design, the mechanics are how you put it together," Al explains. "As a teacher, I stress more the mechanics than the art. The art will come to them naturally, the colors and the choice of flowers and the mixing, but the basic foundations of design are more important, what it is you need to make this whole composition come together. In the first week we cover the seven principles of floral design: balance, accent, proportion, composition, unity, rhythm, and harmony and how they apply to funeral work. We gear the second week to using these principles and how they apply to everyday arrangements and party work. The third week we go into wedding work."

For further training, students attend seminars and workshops sponsored by local wholesalers or the AIFD, the American Institute of Floral Design, which is the professional association to which floral designers strive to belong. But admission to this organization is very competitive.

Admission to the AIFD

Many floral designers, once they complete their training and have packed enough on-the-job experience under their belts, choose to apply for admission to the American Institute of Floral Designers. Membership in AIFD is very selective and candidates must fulfill rigid qualifications and demonstrate advanced design ability.

The process of admission has two phases. In Phase I candidates must submit a portfolio of their work, which includes photographs in seven specific categories: funeral design, hospital arrangement, dining table arrangement, holiday arrangement, bridal bouquet, their own specialty, and plans for a special wedding or party.

In Phase II candidates must demonstrate their design ability on site at various locations around the country determined by the AIFD. During a three-hour period, candidates complete designs in four categories: funeral arrangement, attendant's bouquet, arrangement for a business opening, and an interpretive design.

These floral design competitions add to a designer's prestige and upgrade the entire floriculture industry. Successful candidates earn the right to be distinguished by the letters "AIFD" after their name.

Salaries for Floral Designers

Although salaries vary in different parts of the country, entry-level floral designers with little or no experience can expect to earn minimum wage to $5 or $6 an hour. "In the flower business," Al Mendoza explains, "you're paid according to productivity and your design ability. Someone who is a good, fast, productive designer can make more money. It can go up to $8, $9, or $10 an hour. Then when you move up into management positions, your salary goes up from there. Your pay scale is not based on how much schooling you've had or how much you know, but how much and how well you actually do."

Commentators

Al Mendoza, in addition to his long list of credits—florist, floral designer, assistant director, and teacher at the American Floral Art School—is also a sought-after commentator at various national, state, and local flower shows. Some of the shows are open to the public, others are geared to floral industry professionals.

"At a show, four or five designers from different flower shops create their arrangements, which are then brought to the stage. I comment on them for the audience. If it's a public show, I tell them about the design, the names of the flowers, flower care, the uses of this particular design. If it's for a floral group, then I talk about the mechanics, how this particular design was made.

"If it's a competition, I might be asked to also judge the arrangements, but the judging is not done on stage, it's done behind closed doors."

Al is asked to commentate all over the country and in the Far East. Most commentators are full-time floral designers or teachers and are recognized in the field. Commentators are paid anywhere from $200 to $500 a day plus expenses.

Plant Crafts

Plant lovers with a knack for handicrafts can add to their earnings by fashioning and selling a variety of specialty items utilizing plants.

At Christmas time, front door wreathes and arrangements of mistletoe for hanging and holly leaves for corsages are very popular. Dried flower arrangements do well at any time of the year, as do fragrant potpourri sachets filled with flowers, herbs, spices, and essential oils. David Hirsch, in his book *The Moose-wood Restaurant Kitchen Garden*, (discussed in depth in Chapter Seven) provides recipes and these and other tips for creating long-lasting potpourri:

"Pick flowers for potpourri early in the day, after the dew has dried. Flowers should be in bud or just beginning to open, but not in full bloom or past their prime. Dry them on a screen in a warm, well-ventilated spot out of direct sunlight until they are just brittle. Use recently dried herbs and freshly ground spices for additional fragrance. Store potpourri in covered, nonmetallic containers to retain the fragrance."

Selling Your Crafts

Craftspeople sell their wares through a variety of outlets. They utilize mail-order catalogs or make arrangements for consignments with florists or crafts shops. They frequent arts and crafts fairs or sell to customers through word of mouth.

How much they earn depends on the amount of time each item takes to make, the cost of materials (generally low), and retail store markups or commissions.

Interiorscaping

Interiorscapers study an inside setting, such as a hotel atrium or office building lobby, and with their clients' preferences in mind, choose the best plants for the lighting and temperature conditions as well as for their aesthetic value. Although an in-depth knowledge of plants is crucial, interiorscapers must have a very strong sense of design, much as an architect does.

This interesting career is covered in depth in Chapter Three.

Further Reading

Opportunities in Horticulture Careers, by Jan Goldberg, NTC Publishing.

PFD—Professional Floral Design, *Floral Finance*, and *Retail Florist* are three monthlies available through AFS, P.O. Box 12309, Oklahoma City, OK 73157.

For Further Information

American Association of Nurserymen
1250 Eye St., N.W., Ste. 500
Washington, D.C. 20005

Jim Behrens, Director of Educational Programs
American Floral Services, Inc.
P.O. Box 12309
Oklahoma City, OK 73157

American Floral Art School
529 South Wabash Ave., #600
Chicago, IL 60605-1679

American Floral Services
P.O. Box 12309
Oklahoma City, OK 73157

American Florists Association
2525 Heathcliff
Reston, VA 22091

American Institute of Floral Designers
720 Light St.
Baltimore, MD 21230-3816

Society of American Florists
1601 Duke St.
Alexandria, VA 22314-3406

The Lay of the Land

Design, Maintenance, and Conservation

T he United States is filled with beautiful greenery, from the well-manicured lawns in suburban neighborhoods to public and privately owned parks and forests. To design and maintain these areas a growing number of residential, commercial, and government clients rely on the services of a wide range of horticultural, landscape, forestry, and conservation specialists.

.These specialists have the task of planning and caring for all kinds of land areas, paying attention to conservation and the impact on the environment as well as aesthetics.

Job Titles for Land Design and Maintenance

Job titles range from those open to the unskilled laborer, with little or no experience and training in horticulture, to the master's-degree-level professional, as well as all the steps in between. This chapter will examine the following careers and job titles:

Land Planners

Landscape Architects

Landscape Archaeology

Landscape Designers

Supervisors and Directors

Gardeners and Groundskeepers

Pesticide Technicians

Historic Landscape Preservation

Topiary Training

Golf Course Management

Interiorscapers

Plant Sitters

Conservationists

Foresters

Job Settings for Land Design and Maintenance

Work is available almost anywhere you see a tree, a shrub, or a lawn. Job seekers don't have to scour help wanted ads or move across the country to find employment (although doing so could help broaden the scope). Just look around you at all the possibilities. Each of the following settings requires a range of workers:

Arboreta

Athletic fields

Botanical gardens

Cemeteries

Golf courses

Highways

Historic areas

Hospitals

Hotels

Museums

Office buildings

Playgrounds

Private homes

Public parks and gardens

Recreational facilities

Shopping malls

Theme parks

University campuses

Land Planners

Land planners work in urban or rural settings devising plans that best utilize a community's land. They are knowledgeable about zoning and building codes and environmental regulations. Before preparing plans for long-range development, land planners conduct detailed studies that show the current use. These reports include information concerning the location of streets, highways, water and sewer lines, public buildings, and recreational sites. This information allows them to propose ways of using undeveloped or underutilized land. Land planners then recommend layouts of buildings and other facilities such as subway lines and stations. Land planners also have to show how the plans will be carried out and what they will cost.

Land planners divide their time between office work and on-site inspections. They also attend meetings and public hearings with citizens' groups.

Employment for Land Planners

Two out of three land planners work for government planning agencies, from local cities and counties to state and federal agencies. Some of these agencies include the Department of Defense, Housing and Urban Development, and the Department of Transportation.

Other planners do consulting work or work full-time for firms that provide services to private developers or government agencies. Private sector employers include management and public relations firms, architecture and surveying firms, educational institutions, and large land developers. Salaries vary depending upon the hiring institution and the amount of education a land planner has pursued. Annual averages run $39,000 for bachelor's degree holders, $43,000 for those with a master's degree, and $57,000 for doctorate holders.

What It Takes to Be a Land Planner

Land planners, in addition to their training in planning, landscape architecture, and civil engineering, must also be diplomats with excellent communication skills. Land planners work and interact with a variety of related professionals including architects, city managers, environmental engineers, and geographers. They must also be able to negotiate with groups who may oppose the proposed development.

Landscape Architecture

Landscape architecture is the design of outside areas that are beautiful, functional, and compatible with the natural environment. A landscape architect can work with small residential or commercial projects, or with complex projects on a much larger scale. These could include projects for cities or counties, industrial parks, historical sites, and a variety of other settings.

Training for Landscape Architects

A bachelor's or master's degree is usually necessary for entry into the profession. Many Bachelor's of Landscape Architecture (BLA) programs take five years to complete; a master's degree can take two or three years. The two-year master's program is designed for bachelor's level landscape architects; the three-year program is for people with a bachelor's degree in a field other than landscape architecture.

Your college curriculum will include the following courses:

History of landscape architecture

Landscape design and construction

Landscape ecology

Structural design

Drafting

Urban and regional planning

Design and color theory

Soil science

Geology

Meteorology

Topography

Plant science and other introductory horticulture courses

Civil engineering, including grading and drainage and pipe design

Construction law and contracts

General management

Going on for a master's degree will help refine your design abilities, focusing on more complex types of design problems. It will also add greatly to your employability and salary prospects.

Almost all of the 50 states require landscape architects to be licensed. Licensing is based on passing the Landscape Architect Registration Examination (LARE) sponsored by the Council of Landscape Architecture Registration Boards. Admission to the exam usually requires a college degree and from one to four years or more of work experience. Some states such as Florida and Arizona require an additional exam focusing on the laws or plant materials indigenous to that state.

Landscape architects employed by the federal government are not required to be licensed.

Before licensing, a new hire will typically be called a landscape architect intern. The title is misleading, however, because interns can, depending upon their employer's requirements, perform all the duties of a licensed landscape architect. But the intern will work under the guidance of a licensed practitioner until he or she has passed the exam.

Salaries for Landscape Architects

Statistics are limited but in 1992 salaries for entry level bachelor's degree landscape architects started out at about $20,400 per year. Those with a master's degree were able to add another $10,000 to their annual salary.

Landscape Design

A landscape designer works similarly to a landscape architect, but usually on residential or small commercial projects. Landscape designers are not technically certified and cannot call themselves landscape architects.

For those who do not wish to invest the number of years it takes to become a landscape architect, a career in landscape design could be the answer. To become a landscape designer you can usually do so after taking a two-year associate's degree in a landscape specialist program offered at a number of schools throughout the country.

Salaries are generally less for designers than for architects, but those who are self-employed are not as limited as those employed by a landscape architecture firm.

Historic Landscape Preservation

Historic landscape preservation is a field of growing interest throughout the country among managers of historic buildings and cultural and natural landscapes. The Colonial Williamsburg

Foundation in Williamsburg, Virginia is one of the largest employers of landscape architects, designers, and related grounds-keeping professionals.

A Close-Up Look at Colonial Williamsburg

Visitors to Colonial Williamsburg meet historical figures, witness events, and participate in the daily lives of the people who helped bring about American independence.

For 81 years, from 1699 to 1780, Williamsburg was the thriving capital of Virginia, one of the original 13 colonies. After the American Revolution, when the capital was moved to Richmond, Williamsburg began a decline that lasted 146 years. It became a sleepy southern town with crumbling roads and buildings, overgrown gardens—and only a distant memory of patriots and prosperity.

In 1926, with his love of American history and a belief that anything is possible, John D. Rockefeller, Jr. began the Colonial Williamsburg restoration project to return this once important city to its former glory.

Now, after over 60 years of work, 88 original eighteenth- and early nineteenth-century structures have been completely re-stored and over 500 others have been reconstructed on original foundations. Colonial gardens have also been recreated, dupli-cating the plants used during the eighteenth century. And beautiful three- and four-hundred-year-old trees still stand, lining the hard-packed dirt walkways.

All of this restoration was accomplished only after extensive archeological and historical investigation.

Landscape Architecture at Colonial Williamsburg

Kent Brinkley is a landscape architect and garden historian at Colonial Williamsburg. He has been with the Foundation for more than ten years.

Kent talks about his job: "I wear a lot of different hats. I sit at a drawing board and I do designs for new work that's taking place. We also have lots of gardens that were designed during the 1930s and '40s by my predecessors, Arthur Shurcliff and Alden Hopkins. They did a lot of research and picked plants that were known and used in the eighteenth century. But in a few cases, a plant they chose, even though it was appropriate to the period, might not have been happy in a specific location because of too much sunlight or too much shade. So we try to come up with something else that would have been used but will grow better and flourish in that specific location.

"Many of these gardens are getting on in years. They're 40 or 50 years old and, unlike the architecture where you just replace fabric when a board rots or you're putting a coat of paint on, plant materials do grow. They're dynamic and when you have a garden that's mature, or overmature as many of ours happen to be, part of my charge is looking at the replacements that inevitably have to be factored in when plants or trees die out. This keeps it looking presentable to the public.

"I work closely with Bob Scott (introduced later in this chapter) who is responsible for the maintenance. I provide the design expertise and we talk about what is needed in a particular garden. Once a decision has been made, Bob directs his main-tenance staff to implement the work.

"I also spend time giving slide lectures to groups and garden clubs. I give garden tours a couple of times a month to the public just to have contact with the visitors on the street.

"I'm also a garden historian. That is someone who has a background in history and has done research and is interested in the development of the historical landscape over time. I've made any number of trips to England in the last 14 or 15 years and have visited many country estates and gardens over there. I've looked at English landscape design which served as the precedent for many of the designs in the eighteenth century here in the Virginia Colony. Much of my work involves looking at what was done historically in gardens. The kinds of plants that were grown, how they were laid out, the types of fencing they were using—it's all part of knowing how to recreate a period garden.

"It's a specialty someone comes to within a history curriculum. It's a young field in this country; it didn't start as a discipline until 1975. If this interests you, you would combine history courses with horticulture courses. Of course, the job market is fairly small, but it's growing. Right now most jobs are at living history museums such as Williamsburg, or Sturbridge Village and Plimoth Plantation in Massachusetts.

"When I got my job at Williamsburg I was ecstatic. This was the perfect marriage of my love of history and my work as a landscape architect. It's been wonderful to be able to take two major interests and combine them in a way that allows you to do both."

Landscape Archaeology

"There is a new discipline called landscape archaeology," Kent Brinkley explains. "The purpose is to recover enough evidence to recreate a garden that existed on the site in a given historical period. Landscape archaeology uses traditional archaeological technique to recover the fence lines, planting beds, and other evidence.

"Part of my job is to work in concert with archaeologists when they're doing excavations on a particular site. Right now a summer field school from the College of William and Mary is going on and we're excavating a garden in town. I'm interested in what they'll find there because this particular site was the home of Saint George Tucker, a fairly prominent Virginian in the eighteenth century whose papers have survived. We know a good bit about his interest in gardening and the things he was growing so we're all very curious to see what the archaeology will turn up, if we find any physical evidence of his garden. We're digging in the spot where the original garden was. We expect to find evidence of pathways, fence lines and post holes—they leave a definite dark stain. We can also find planting beds and outbuilding foundations, brick foundations of dairies and chicken coops.

"When you excavate the soil from the planting bed, you sometimes find seed materials in the soil samples. You screen the soil and take it into a lab. There's a method known as flotation which separates the water from the soil, and any minute particles, seeds, and things, can be recovered. Then using a microscope you can identify the type of plant from the seed. We can also do pollen analysis. But it's problematical because you don't always know how the seeds ended up in the bed. They could have been dropped by birds or blown by wind.

"But with phytolith analysis we can solve that problem. Phytolith analysis looks at the mineralized tissues of plants. A plant absorbs water and minerals through its root system. When a plant dies the liquid material will crystallize, and when it does, it takes on an impression of the plant cell wall structure. Then all the phytoliths are deposited in the soil as the plant decays. So, unlike seeds or pollen, which could have gotten there for a number of reasons, when you find phytolith in the soil sample, you can be 99 percent certain the plant was actually grown there and didn't just happen."

Just as with gardening history, there is no particular university degree at this time in landscape archaeology. To become a landscape archaeologist you have to follow a traditional program in anthropology and archaeology. Then, once you graduate and start getting on-the-job experience, you can specialize.

Kent's Background

Kent Brinkley has a BA in history from Mary Baldwin College in Staunton, Virginia. "I'm a dying breed—you see it less and less. But I came to landscape architecture through the back door. Just as lawyers used to be able to read the law under a licensed practitioner and then sit for the bar exam, years ago you used to be able to apprentice in a landscape architecture office under a licensed practitioner. It was an equal time commitment. In other words, when you got a five year BLA degree, you generally had to work in an office three years before you could sit for the exam. Or in lieu of that you could do eight years in an office and then take the exam. I waited 10 years before I took the exam.

"I started as a draftsman and worked my way up to vice president of the firm before coming to Williamsburg."

Some Advice for Future Landscape Architects

Kent Brinkley offers the following suggestions:

"People who are mechanically inclined or are curious how things fit together and work would probably find landscape architecture and drafting to their liking. There is a lot of drafting involved; you have to know how to cultivate that drawing talent. You can get a leg up on the competition that way.

"You also have to have good English skills. You need the ability to write and speak well because you're working with people every day. You might have to get up in front of a group and make a presentation to sell your designs. Some sales ability is a good thing to have; you have to market yourself, your firm, and the design, and be able to persuade people that this is the way to go. You can never waste your time by taking additional English or drawing courses.

"And I always advise students that once they've graduated they should work in several different offices and get different kinds of experiences for the first five or six years. It's not a good idea to lock yourself into any one place. Some people study landscape architecture but they don't know what facet they want to pursue. They need time to test the waters before they'll know what their niche will be.

"And it's my personal recommendation to anyone coming into the field to work for two or three years before taking the licensing exam. It's comprehensive in scope and tests you on a variety of things. You need to get some experience under your belt before you try to tackle it.

"To conclude, I can tell students I think there's a bright future in the twenty-first century. For years the architects have beat their chests and said we're the guys who are going to save the world, but they haven't. They've done some pretty wretched designs. And then the engineers said they could do it, and though they certainly design functional work, they seem to have no feeling for aesthetics. So, now, there's a growing awareness that landscape architects may be the people to include on the design team. We are the ones who have a broad enough range of expertise to worry about environmental concerns and other things to make the resulting projects user-friendly and earth-friendly."

Gardening and Groundskeeping

While landscape architects and related professionals are the ones who develop the designs, it's the gardeners and groundskeepers who implement the plans and maintain the work.

They find employment at all of the sites mentioned at the beginning of this chapter, planting, pruning, mowing, transplanting, fertilizing, spraying, trimming, training, edging, and performing any other duties to keep the landscape healthy and beautiful looking.

Meet Bob Scott, Director of Landscape Services at Colonial Williamsburg

Bob Scott has worked in horticulture all his life. He studied music at the College of William and Mary and has a teaching certificate. He also took horticultural courses at Penn State.

"Horticulture was what was helping to pay my way through my music studies," Bob explains. "But then I decided that maybe being a public school music teacher was not what I wanted to do. I had a small greenhouse operation in Norfolk so I decided to expand in that area."

Bob has been at Colonial Williamsburg 22 years. He has 70 or so full-time employees who work around the calendar year.

Bob describes the duties of the different positions he supervises: "The entry level positions are groundskeepers; then we have a gardening ladder, Gardener A, Gardener B, Gardener C; then senior gardener. We go from there to foreman, who covers a particular area, and then we have supervisors who manage three or more foremen. These supervisors report directly to me.

"The Groundskeeper position is basically a nonskilled labor position. He is brought on board to supply the gardening staff with the brawn to clean up and take care of things. We are not interested in his being a skillful person, though we find many of them are worth training to be promoted.

"Gardener A is the entry level position on the gardening ladder. This job requires a minimum of skills. For instance, Gardener A would have to know the difference between perennials and annuals, have some general knowledge of pruning and turf maintenance, and some basic knowledge of chemicals, pesticides, herbicides, and fungicides, though he's not required to use them. But, to be promoted to a Gardener B, he would have to become a certified technician by the requirements of the State of Virginia.

"Gardener B is at a more professional level. He would have a technician's license for the use of pesticides. He would not have to have a college degree but he would have to be able to figure the math for the use of chemicals. Gardener B does all gardening chores and landscape maintenance, watering, pruning, fertilizing, planting, transplanting, bed working, and edging.

"Gardener C would have a commercial pesticide license and can then supervise those under him. He would have the responsibility for some groundskeepers working under him and would be responsible for a geographic area under his direction.

"A Senior Gardener works very similarly to a C gardener but he has more responsibility. He would make sure the other team members have the material and equipment they would need to do their work. And he would also fill in for the foreman if he were on vacation or out sick, running the crews and doing the time cards.

"The Foreman position is in charge of a team that takes care of a large geographic area. A C gardener might be confined to seven pieces of property, for example, but a foreman might have 15. The foreman should have a college degree but it's not mandatory.

"I have three Supervisors who report directly to me. They take care of the business properties, the museum properties, and the historic properties.

"My job as director is to keep the three supervisors in line. In reality, although it doesn't say so in the job description, I deal with all the personnel problems for the department. I enjoy doing that because I'm a gardener at heart and I know the kind of problems the gardeners have. My three supervisors are college people with bachelor's and master's degrees in botany and horticulture, but they haven't necessarily had the same exposure to what it's like being a gardener the way I have."

Bob reports to the Director of Landscape and Facility Services who has several other departments that report directly to him just as Bob does.

Bob also works closely with Kent Brinkley, Williamsburg's resident landscape architect and landscape historian.

Meet a Topiary Trainer at Colonial Williamsburg

One of Bob Scott's employees is Wesley Greene. Wesley is a landscape supervisor at Colonial Williamsburg and oversees the maintenance of the Historic Area gardens. He is also a licensed arborist in charge of the tree crew. His special interest is topiary.

Wesley talks about his job: "I started in the green industry in 1978, working in summer jobs through high school. I worked for the National Park Service, college campuses, and private industry. I have a bachelor's degree in botany from the University of Maine and I've been at Williamsburg since 1981.

"Basically my function is to train others, to give them the technical support, or sometimes a kick, whichever is required. I oversee the maintenance, supervising 26 gardeners and tree surgeons, and I do some design and most of the topiary layout. Occasionally I do some of the actual topiary work myself because I enjoy it.

A Lesson in Topiary

Wesley describes the art of topiary: "Topiary comes from the Latin word *topiarius*, which then meant ornamental gardener. It first arose during the Roman era. The first time the word topiary appeared referring to a plant training technique as opposed to the gardener was in an engraving of an arbor.

"The art of topiary is the shaping of plants. A hedge is a piece of topiary. We tend to think of animals or geometric shapes as topiary, but, really, any shape on a plant such as a trimmed hedge would qualify.

"There are two different kinds of topiary: those formed using wire structures, as you see at Disney theme parks, and those formed without wire structures. Ladew Gardens in Maryland is one of the best examples of horses and fox hunts and those are true topiaries formed without wires.

"At Disney they use a wire form and let the plant grow around it, continuing to shape it as it grows. We don't use wire forms at Williamsburg. We start with the plant and grow it into a shape.

"Williamsburg has 178 acres of formal gardens, hedges, free-standing pieces and topiary pieces that are incorporated into hedges. We have *estrade* topiary, which is a big gumball shape in a layer cake design with a series of disks. Throughout Williamsburg you'll see lots of squares, domes, and circles. Some flat top hedges on the corners will have bubbles on top or diamond shapes. Some hedges sweep up at the corners.

"It's all based on eighteenth-century landscaping. By the middle of the 1700s animal topiary was considered to be vulgar and you won't see any animal shapes at Williamsburg.

"To train topiary you shear as you make the shape you want, but you have to keep a compact plant structure so it holds itself up in wind, rain, and snow, at the same time maintaining a straight central trunk. That's critical. If you lose the trunk you have to start over. Once we have overall shape we lay it out. This is the Wesley Greene method; I use a little algebra here. I believe there's beauty in mathematics. There's a saying I made up: Formality by definition is wedded to geometry, and geometry by natural law is insufferable to approximation.

"That means you're exactly right or you don't show up.

"If you follow things mathematically, the eye picks up the repetition. Repetition sounds like a boring word but it's the hallmark of good landscape design, repeating the forms, colors, and shapes throughout the garden design, or with topiary, within the individual piece.

"Although topiary is as old as the Roman Empire, it really got going much later in Holland. William and Mary brought it with them to England, but to excess. It got to the point on the big estates such as Hampton Court and Blenheim that every tree and every plant was made into a squirrel or circle or box and it was those excesses that brought the art down. And you can imagine how difficult and expensive it was keeping those gardens maintained.

"Just before the middle of the eighteenth century, the first move toward naturalism began, where you'd have a grove of trees, and a lake and a broad beautiful vista. In Europe the landowners were going broke at the time, so this new movement came in and everyone started ripping out their formal gardens.

"We think topiary lasted in this country a little longer. It had sentimental value, what gardens looked like in their home countries in Europe. And also, being in the midst of a vast wilderness in the new world, there was something to be said about taking a piece of land and making it behave. People are at the mercy of nature and they respond by trying to control it. It's an insecure way of gardening."

Golf Course Management

Golf is the only major sport without a standardized playing field. Every golf course has unique features, from its architecture to the different ecosystems and microenvironments found across its acreage. Because of this, golf course managers have to be skilled in a number of disciplines.

Below are descriptions of the different golf course related jobs that would be of interest to plant lovers.

Golf Course Superintendent A golf course's top manager must wear a number of hats. In order to provide a playing surface that meets aesthetic and playing standards as well as preserves environmental integrity, she must be a scientist familiar with agronomy, entomology, soil science, meteorology, chemistry, physics, and more.

The superintendent assumes responsibility for all phases of a golf course's operation including construction and maintenance of the grounds as well as typical administrative duties.

Assistant Golf Course Superintendent The assistant golf course superintendent reports directly to the superintendent. The assistant directs and participates in planning, laying out, and supervising the maintenance of the golf course tees, greens, fairways, and cart paths and other related work.

Horticulturist The horticulturist manages the greenhouse and nursery and selects, propagates, and grows plant materials for the ornamental landscaping for the golf course and clubhouse.

The horticulturist supervises and instructs groundskeepers in routine maintenance.

Irrigation Specialist The irrigation specialist is responsible for programming, operating, and maintaining golf course irrigation systems. He reports any irregularities in course turf quality to the superintendent or assistant.

Chemical Technician The chemical technician performs chemical applications on golf course properties. She must perform routine safety inspections on all spraying equipment and maintain storage areas that meet all county, state, and federal regulations.

Gardener-Triplex Operator The gardener-triplex operator runs light motorized equipment on the golf course in order to perform mowing, sand-trap raking, and other related duties.

Groundskeeper The groundskeeper performs routine manual labor related to golf course management including operating mowers and string trimmers.

Training and Education for Golf Course Personnel

The amount of training and education varies depending upon the position. A groundskeeper, as mentioned earlier, relies more on muscle and minimal knowledge of gardening rather than on college degrees. But the horticulturist and superintendents must have degrees in appropriate fields such as turf management or plant science. Some positions, especially those involving chemicals and pesticides, must be licensed.

For more information about careers and training in golf course management write to the Golf Course Superintendents Association of America. Their address is listed at the end of this chapter.

Interiorscaping

An interiorscaper works with clients who want to create indoor environments filled with plants. The interiorscaper provides the design, oversees the installation, and, if the contract specifies, maintains the health and attractiveness of the layout.

Interiorscapers find work with large landscape contracting firms or nurseries, or they can go it independently, renting space with adequate lighting in a warehouse where they can store their plants. In addition, some large land developers, rather than contracting the work out, hire permanent on-staff interiorscapers to take care of the malls or other complexes they own.

Although private home owners might utilize the services of an interiorscaper, most clients come from the commercial world.

Greg Blackwell, Interiorscaper

Greg Blackwell works for Creative Plantings, a large contracting firm in Burtonsville, Maryland. He talks about the role of an interiorscaper: "We deal with hotels, office buildings, shopping malls, restaurants, corporate headquarters, and other types of both large and small businesses.

"We meet with clients to discuss their needs, what they're looking for. We try to get an idea from them the scope of the work, from a planting standpoint and also their budget. In the initial visit, I try to get as much information as I can to work with: for example, blueprints of the buildings, light readings, colors and accents in the surroundings, types of finishes and furniture styles, and sources of water. In larger jobs the time of year might be important. Because of freezing temperatures you have to protect material from the cold weather during the delivery process.

"Then, if it's possible, we like our clients to visit our facility. We have greenhouses where they can pick out particular plants. We also have photographs we can show them. Depending on the person, he might want to leave it all up to you, or he might prefer to be involved and have a say in it.

"On some jobs, I'll write up specifications, doing detailed drawings and layout, and artist renderings, to show what the space would look like with plants, and the different kinds of containers and finishes. After I work on the plans and have my presentation all ready, I go back and meet with the clients again and see how they feel about it. If they approve the plan, the next step would be to organize obtaining the materials. If we don't have them in stock, then sometimes I have to go directly to the growers, wholesalers, or importers in Florida and select the material and tag the actual plants I'll need.

"Then we schedule delivery and installation and coordinate with the other trades. Interiorscapers are usually the last people in on a project, especially if it's a new building. We have to wait until all the construction is done.

"After the job is installed we usually come back on a weekly schedule and clean the plants and inspect them for any insects or disease. If they're in a situation where the light is coming in strongly from one side, we have to rotate the plants because they start facing toward the sun. And we'll also replace any plants that aren't doing well."

Other duties Greg is responsible for include estimating, monitoring inventory, purchasing, and photographing. The latter skill he uses to chronicle possible plant arrangements for customers and also to enter designs into professional competitions.

The Finances of Interiorscaping

Clients of Creative Plantings have two choices: they can either purchase the plants and containers outright and have a separate maintenance contract they would be billed monthly for, or they can lease the entire package. They would have one monthly payment and a small up-front charge, which involves a smaller overall cash layout.

Creative Plantings offers another service. Greg Blackwell explains: "We provide short-term rentals for conventions and weddings and other types of special events, including a large-scale event such as the inauguration and all the balls here in Washington, D.C."

While interiorscapers with large firms or nurseries usually have a selection of plants already in stock, a self-employed designer could operate with only a small inventory. It is possible, utilizing pictures, to set up a job with a client, and then order the plants needed from a local wholesaler.

Job Titles within the Field of Interiorscaping

Within the field of interiorscaping there are several different job titles: designers, estimators, and operations managers. Interiorscapers utilize the services of installers, delivery people, and job installation supervisors. Maintenance technicians take care of the plants, and maintenance foremen supervise the technicians.

Nurseries who employ interiorscapers also hire competent sales staff to deal with customers.

The chance for advancement is very good within the industry. With some experience under their belts, installers and maintenance technicians, for example, can move up to supervisory positions or into sales.

Training for Interiorscapers

Many people start out already established in the floral business, as florists or floral designers, for example, and interiorscaping then follows, becoming a natural extension of what they're already doing. A flower shop owner might stock tropical house plants for retail. Through walk-in customers from local office buildings, a florist can then be requested to add installation and maintenance to their services.

Greg Blackwell of Creative Plantings is actually a registered landscape architect with a strong interest in interior design. He started with a BS in horticulture from Virginia, specializing in landscape design.

Most interiorscaping programs fall under the auspices of a landscape architecture or landscape design program. Community colleges also offer courses, but a degree is not necessary to pursue a career as an interiorscaper; many firms will take on interns and provide on-the-job training.

Salaries for Interiorscapers

Entry level crew workers and technicians can start anywhere from $6 to $13 or $14 an hour. Someone with a new bachelor's degree could expect to earn in the teens or 20s, depending on the region of the country. Designers and managers earn anywhere from $30,000 to $60,000 per year.

Plant Sitters

Plant sitters work on a scale much smaller than interiorscapers. They are usually self-employed, part-time workers and function much as a babysitter or dog walker would. Plant sitting enables a student, for example, to earn extra money taking care of vacationing neighbors' plants. It's also an excellent way for a student exploring the field of horticulture to get some hands-on experience.

To find work, enterprising plant sitters canvas the neighborhood, knocking door to door. They post notices on community bulletin boards, print up flyers and distribute them in parking lots, hand out business cards, and cultivate word-of-mouth contacts.

Plant sitters should have some experience with plants but it is also likely that the experience will come directly from on-the-job training. Most plant owners hiring the services of a plant sitter will leave explicit instructions for the care of each plant.

Salaries for plant sitters can range from an hourly wage to a flat fee for the time period involved. As a plant sitter's client list grows, so will the amount of money earned.

Foresters and Conservationists

Forests and rangelands serve a variety of needs. They supply wood products, livestock forage, minerals, and water; serve as sites for recreational activities; and provide habitats for wildlife. Foresters and conservation scientists manage, develop, use, and help protect these and other natural resources.

Although many professional foresters and forest technicians spend most of their time working outdoors during the first few years of their career, there are many who do not. Outdoor duties include

Measuring and grading trees

Evaluating insect outbreaks

Conducting land surveys

Fighting wildfires

Laying out road systems

Supervising construction of trails and planting of trees

Supervising timber harvesting

Conducting research studies

After a few years of on-the-ground experience, foresters can advance to administrative positions and then spend less time outside. These duties include

Planning

Contracting

Preparing reports

Managing budgets

Consulting

A professional forester has earned a four-year degree while a forest technician normally holds an associate's degree in forest technology. Professional foresters concentrate on management skills, policy decisions, and the application of ecological concepts. Technicians generally work under a professional forester accomplishing day-to-day tasks.

Range Managers

Range managers, also called range conservationists, range ecologists, or range scientists, manage, improve, and protect rangelands to maximize their use without damaging the environment.

Soil Conservationists

Soil conservationists provide technical assistance to farmers (see more on farming in Chapter Eight) and others concerned with the conservation of soil, water, and related natural resources. They develop programs to get the most use out of the land without damaging it.

Training for Foresters and Conservationists

In high school, future foresters should concentrate on basic mathematics coursework, computer sciences, chemistry, botany, zoology, soil science, ecology, and related social sciences. It is also important to have good writing and public speaking skills.

A college degree is necessary and those with a BS will advance more and earn more than technicians with just an associate's degree.

The Society of American Foresters recognizes 46 universities offering four-year degree programs and 21 universities offering two-year associate's degrees. For a list of these schools contact the Society of American Foresters at the address given at the end of this chapter.

A bachelor's degree in range management or range science is the usual minimum educational requirement for range managers; graduate degrees are required for teaching and research positions.

Very few colleges offer degrees in soil conservation. Most soil conservationists hold degrees in agronomy, general agriculture, or crop or soil science.

Finding a Job in Forestry and Conservation

The following is a partial list provided by the Society of American Foresters for those seeking employment. (For a complete list, write the Society of American Foresters whose address is listed at the end of this chapter.) Send your requests for the following resources to the addresses indicated. Be sure to ask for the most recent issue. You can also find some of these publications at your library.

Conservation Directory is updated annually and lists by states and Canadian provinces the organizations, agencies, and officials concerned with natural resource use and management. The cost is $18 plus $4.85 shipping and handling. Send your request to National Wildlife Federation, 1400 16th St., NW, Washington, D.C. 20036.

The Ultimate Job Finders Computer Software—IBM Compatible Computers, 7215 Oak Ave., River Forest, IL 60305. $59.95 plus $3.75 shipping and handling.

Government Job Finders, Planning/Communications, 7215 Oak Ave., River Forest, IL 60305. $14.95 plus $3.75 shipping and handling.

The Professional's Job Finders, Planning/Communications, 7215 Oak Ave., River Forest, IL 60305. $15.95 plus $3.75 shipping and handling.

The Non-Profits' Job Finders, Planning/Communications, 7215 Oak Ave., River Forest, IL 60305. $13.95 plus $3.75 shipping and handling.

So You Want to be in Forestry?, The Society of American Foresters, 5400 Grosvenor Lane, Bethesda, MD 20814. 40 cents.

Information about Jobs Currently Available

Journal of Forestry is a monthly publication listing both "positions wanted" and "positions available." It is free to SAF members or $55 per year for subscribers. Society of American Foresters, 5400 Grosvenor Lane, Bethesda, MD 20814.

Job Seeker lists vacancies in forestry, forest products, wildlife, fisheries, range, biology, environmental protection and education, recreation, parks, and other natural resource fields. Advertisers include timber industries, forest consultants, nurseries, federal and state agencies, universities, nature centers, and other related organizations. This biweekly costs $60 per year. P.O. Box 16, Warrens, WI 54666.

Environmental Career Focus is an informative newsletter including job research strategies, agency hiring plans, profiles of selected career fields, salary surveys, interviews with employers and successful job seekers, hiring trends, and a question-and-answer column. $10 per year for four issues. Environmental Career Center, P.O. Box 3451, Hampton, VA 23663.

National Park Service

The National Park Service, a bureau under the U.S. Department of the Interior, administers more than 350 sites. These encompass natural and recreational areas across the country including the Grand Canyon, Yellowstone National Park, and Lake Mead.

Because most sites are not located near major cities, serious candidates must, for the most part, be prepared to relocate. Housing may or may not be provided, depending upon the site and your position.

Park Rangers

The National Park Service hires three categories of Park Rangers (generally on a seasonal basis): Enforcement, General, and Interpretation. Most plant lovers apply for positions in the General category.

Duties vary greatly from position to position and site to site, but Rangers in the general division are usually responsible for forestry or resource management, developing and presenting programs that explain a park's historic, cultural, or archaeological features, campground maintenance, firefighting, lifeguarding, law enforcement, and performing search and rescue activities.

Rangers also sit at information desks, provide visitor services or participate in conservation or restoration projects. Entry level employees might also collect fees, provide first aid, and operate audiovisual equipment.

Qualifications and Salaries

In determining a candidate's eligibility for employment, and at which salary level he or she would be placed, the National Park

Service weighs several factors. In essence, those with the least experience or education will begin at the lowest Federal Government salary grade of GS-2. But the requirements for that grade are only six months of experience in related work, or a high school diploma or its equivalency.

The more related work experience or education, the higher the salary level. For example, GS-4 requires 18 months of general experience in park operations or in related fields and 6 months of specialized experience; or one 90-day season as a seasonal Park Ranger at the GS-3 level.

Completion of two academic years of college may be substituted for experience if the coursework covered is related.

Getting Your Foot in the Door

"Competition for jobs, especially at the most well-known sites, can be fierce," explains Gordie Wilson, Superintendent of Castillo de San Marcos National Monument, an historic fort in St. Augustine, Florida. "But the National Park Service employs a huge permanent staff, and this is supplemented ten-fold by an essential seasonal work force during peak visitation periods.

"The best way for a newcomer to break in is to start off with seasonal employment during school breaks. With a couple of summer seasons under your belt, the doors will open more easily for permanent employment."

Because of Office of Personnel Management regulations, veterans of the U.S. Armed Forces have a decided advantage. Depending upon their experience, they may be given preference among applicants.

How to Apply

Recruitment for summer employment begins September 1 with a January 15 deadline. Some sites such as Death Valley or Everglades National Park also have a busy winter season. The winter recruitment period is June 1 through July 15.

Applications for seasonal employment with the National Park service can be obtained through the Office of Personnel Management or by writing to the U.S. Department of the Interior,

National Park Service, Seasonal Employment Unit, P.O. Box 37127, Washington, D.C. 20013-7127.

You may also contact one of the 10 regional offices of the National Park Service. Their addresses are listed in Appendix B.

Further Reading

Careers for Nature Lovers, Louise Miller, NTC Publishing.

Opportunities in Forestry Careers, Christopher M. Wille, NTC Publishing.

For Further Information

American Forestry Association
P.O. Box 2000
Washington, D.C. 20013

American Landscape Horticulture Association
2509 E. Thousand Oaks Blvd., Ste. # 109
Westlake Village, CA 91362

American Planning Association
1776 Massachusetts Ave., N.W.
Washington, D.C. 20036

American Society of Landscape Architects
4401 Connecticut Ave. N.W., 5th Fl.
Washington, D.C. 20008-2302

Associated Landscape Contractors of America, Inc.
405 N. Washington St., #104
Falls Church, VA 22046

Association of Professional Landscape Designers
P.O. Box 134
Kensington, MD 20895

Bureau of Land Management
U.S. Department of the Interior
Room 3619
1849 C Street, N.W.
Washington, D.C. 20240

Colonial Williamsburg
Employment Office
P.O. Box 1776
Williamsburg, VA 23187

Council of Landscape Architectural Registration Boards
12700 Fair Lakes Circle, Ste. 110
Fairfax, VA 22033

Council of Tree and Landscape Appraisers
1250 I St., N.W., Ste. 504
Washington, D.C. 20005

Earth Work
Student Conservation Association
Box 550 Charlestown, NH 03603

Golf Course Superintendents Association of America
1421 Research Park Dr.
Lawrence, KS 66049-3859

National Landscape Association
1250 Eye St., N.W. #500
Washington, D.C. 20005

National Park Service
U.S. Department of the Interior
P.O. Box 37127
Washington, D.C. 20013-7127

The National Pest Control Association
250 West Jersey St.
Elizabeth, NJ 07207

National Wildlife Federation
1400 16th St., N.W.
Washington, D.C. 20036

Professional Grounds Management Society
10402 Ridgland Rd., Ste. 4
Hunt Valley, MD 21030

Society of American Foresters
5400 Grosvenor Ln.
Bethesda, MD 20814

U.S. Forest Service
U.S. Department of Agriculture
14th St. and Independence Ave., S.W.
Washington, D.C. 20250

World Forestry Center
4033 S.W. Canyon Rd.
Portland, OR 97221

CHAPTER FOUR

Botanical Gardens and Arboreta

Botanical gardens and arboreta (the plural of arboretum) are parks open to the general public, students, and research scientists. Plants, flowers, trees, and shrubs are collected from all over the world and exhibited in arrangements by family, country of origin, or aesthetics.

Typical visitors to botanical gardens and arboreta generally fall into six categories: dedicated professional scientists and horticulturalists who utilize the gardens' collections for research purposes or to identify specific plants; professional and amateur gardeners who participate in adult education classes and training programs; horticultural students enrolled in internship programs through their universities; local residents who come to enjoy a peaceful sanctuary; schoolchildren and their teachers; and international travelers and scientists interested in the collections and history of the gardens.

Botanical gardens and arboreta generally offer public programs such as classes in gardening, question-and-answer hotlines to help with gardening problems, tours of the grounds, and lectures on the various collections.

Although not all, most botanical gardens and arboreta are involved with ongoing research issues. Curators and other horticulturists go on collection trips to add to the types of plants in their gardens and to study the plant life in other geographic regions.

Living plants are added to the grounds and pressed and dried plants are stored in herbaria and are shared with researchers all over the world.

The Different Jobs Within

Horticulture Department Organization Chart

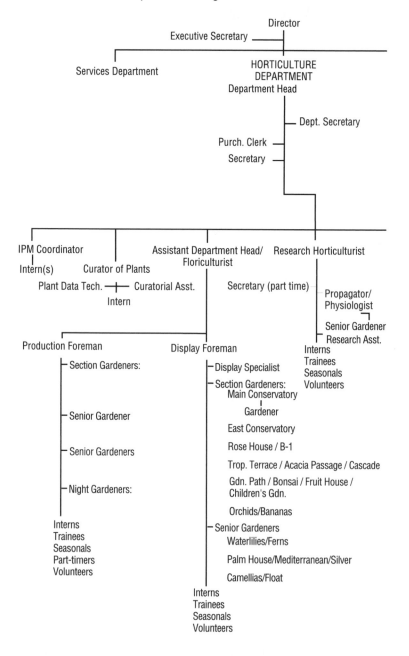

Botanical Garens and Arboreta

Maintenance Department

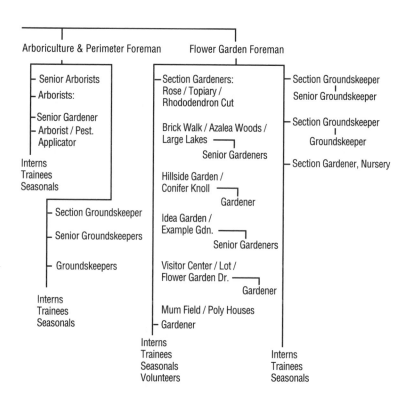

Arboriculture & Perimeter Foreman

- Senior Arborists
- Arborists:

- Senior Gardener
- Arborist / Pest.
  Applicator

Interns
Trainees
Seasonals

- Section Groundskeeper

- Senior Groundskeepers

- Groundskeepers

Interns
Trainees
Seasonals

Flower Garden Foreman

- Section Gardeners:
  Rose / Topiary /
  Rhododendron Cut

Brick Walk / Azalea Woods /
Large Lakes
    Senior Gardeners

Hillside Garden /
Conifer Knoll
    Gardener

Idea Garden /
Example Gdn.
    Senior Gardeners

Visitor Center / Lot /
Flower Garden Dr.
    Gardener

Mum Field / Poly Houses
- Gardener

Interns
Trainees
Seasonals
Volunteers

- Section Groundskeeper
  Senior Groundskeeper

- Section Groundskeeper
  Groundskeeper

- Section Gardener, Nursery

Interns
Trainees
Seasonals

Salaries with Botanical Gardens and Arboreta

A chart showing average salaries for selected job titles is below. The geographic region, the size and budget of the institution, and the experience of the applicant will all determine actual salaries, which could be far greater or lower than these averages.

SELECTED JOB TITLES, DUTIES, AND APPROXIMATE AVERAGE ANNUAL SALARIES

Position	Job Description	Salary
Administration, Facilities, Security		
Director	Provides leadership and is responsible for policy making, funding, planning, organizing, staffing, and directing activities throughout the institution.	$48,000
Assistant Director	Has general responsibility for operations, which may include finance, personnel, and maintenance of facilities, security, and safety.	$40,000
Business Manager	Is responsible for accounting, payroll and benefits, purchasing, personnel, and financial record keeping.	$32,190
Store Manager	Manage's the institution's gift shop or store.	$22,000
Security Officer	Guards property against theft, illegal entry, fire, and vandalism. Enforces rules and regulations, protects visitors, and may be required to administer first aid.	$20,280
Horticulture, Curation of Collections		
Head of Horticulture	Directs the horticultural function of the institution including the management of staff, programs, activities, and plant collections.	$31,100

SELECTED JOB TITLES, DUTIES, AND
APPROXIMATE AVERAGE ANNUAL SALARIES

Position	Job Description	Salary
Curator of Horticulture	Advises on care of plant collections and acquisitions.	$28,180
Plant Records Keeper	Maintains inventory of plants. Processes acquisitions, accession and deaccession, mapping, relocating, and labeling.	$23,675
Horticultural Production Supervisor	Supervises the growing of plants in the nursery.	$23,900
Propagator	Propagates plant materials for collections.	$22,775
	Grounds Management	
Horticulture Supervisor	Supervises garden workers, plans and schedules work assignments, and is responsible for equipment.	$27,000
Foremen	Directs laborer crews in general groundskeeping tasks.	$23,500
Laborer	Maintains general grounds.	$17,470
Gardener	Responsible for the maintenance of a specialized plant area or collection.	$21,254
Arborist	Responsible for the care of trees including trimming, transplanting, and removing.	$21,254
	Education, Visitor Services	
Head of Education	Responsible for several departments or programs. Supervises several education professionals and/or volunteers.	$29,000
Education Specialist	Responsible for a specific program. Supervises staff related to that program.	$23,650
Visitor Services Manager	Coordinates informational programs and services.	$24,460

Rick Darke, Curator of Plants at Longwood Gardens

Longwood Gardens is located in Kennett Square, Pennsylvania, a suburb of Philadelphia. Curator of plants, Rick Darke, explains its function: "We're not really a botanic garden; we're a display garden, a pleasure garden. We have quite a few plants that could be called collections, but they exist for the sake of the landscape texture. That's how we differ from a traditional botanical garden. We have a lot more emphasis on the art of the landscape, the pleasure derived by people being in that landscape, than we have people coming to study these plants as objects.

"A botanical garden is usually a garden whose primary emphasis is collecting plants, keeping data on them for the purpose of display and study.

"Pierre Dupont, the founder of Longwood Gardens, was interested in creating a mood and a sense of place that would allow people to interact within a garden setting. Even though he had a lot of unusual and great specimens, his main emphasis was on the art of horticulture and the setting he was creating. At a botanical garden they worry secondly how well the spaces work for art or entertainment.

"We do have a research division at Longwood within our horticultural division, but our research is not at the micro level. In other words, we're not doing research on projects useful only in laboratory settings or that would not have much practical applicability. What we're trying to do is bring science to bear on display horticulture. We do have true PhD scientists in our division but they're here to use their knowledge of science to help us be efficient, imaginative, and responsible to the environment in our fabricating of plant displays.

"It's a historic garden in some sense. There was an arboretum here started by a Quaker family who got the land from a grant from William Penn, who Pennsylvania is named for. They planted trees in the 1780s that are still existing today and it was that core arboretum that was the compelling factor in Pierre Dupont's decision to buy the property. The trees were due to be logged and Dupont bought the land to save them. He fell in love with the place and over the years developed Longwood Gardens around it.

"Pierre Dupont was an engineer who had a love of water in the garden, so he built fountain gardens which were inspired by his visits to Europe. These are major attractions. We also have a theater garden with live performances. The curtain is a curtain of water jets.

"There's also a topiary garden of abstract shapes and lots of wonderful old trees, grand vistas, and monumental architecture at the conservatories, with bronze windows and mica-shaded lamps inside.

"We intend it to be gorgeous and I think we succeed. We wow people in a very classy way."

Rick Darke's Duties as Curator of Plants

Longwood Gardens has a little over 1,000 acres, of that there are about 250 acres accessible to the public, and of that about 80 acres are actually display gardens.

Rick Darke has been at Longwood Gardens for close to 18 years. He talks about his job: "I'm a plantsman for Longwood, someone who is knowledgeable about the diversity of plants that exists in the world because we grow plants from the world over. First and foremost, if there is any one thing that has to get done here, we keep everything at Longwood identified and labeled and that's the most important thing. I organize and oversee the identification, mapping, and labeling that is done by the curatorial assistants I supervise.

"I also have a very steady role in making recommendations and working in team settings to make and refine and restore the gardens at Longwood. To that end, I participate regularly on landscape and advisory committees. My role is to suggest plants we could use in place of what we're using now, or sometimes it overlaps into related areas. I'm often making comments on architectural details or labeling and other interpretive details.

"I also get to travel a lot looking for new plants for Longwood. I've traveled to Australia, New Zealand, Japan, South Africa, Brazil, England, Germany. I bring back beautiful plants from all kinds of climates. We have four acres under glass here so we can grow things that are hardy and we can also create specialized environments that provide the essentials of the environment the plants are from.

"I do quite a bit of teaching, it's a considerable part of the job. We have a lot of different student programs here and I regularly teach a botany course for our PG (Professional Gardener) students, and other classes for our graduate student program. I teach courses for our continuing education program, which includes evening lectures and field trips. I lead tours to native areas and other gardens.

"I also write. I contribute to our inhouse publication, which is essentially a record of the employees and happenings around the garden, and I also write articles for magazines on what Longwood is doing. For example, when I went to Brazil I worked with a landscape architect there and brought him back to Longwood. He made a garden for us and I wrote an article on that. I worked with our photographer to get that published. It's a celebration of the gardens at Longwood."

Rick is a member of the Garden Writers Association of America and is the author of *For Your Garden: Ornamental Grasses* (Little Brown).

The eclectic mix of his job and the interaction he gets to have with students is what Rick likes most about his work. "We usually have an intern in our office and I'm constantly teaching people as they move through the organization. Over the years you can imagine the wonderful network you make of friends and professional colleagues around the country and around the world.

"In my job I get to do something that's fun. It's not just going to work at eight and ending at five. It's much more than that. It really is something that teaches you. I have become in these past 18 years someone who loves his garden at home. I'm out there digging and planting and designing and it's gotten to the point that features of the garden are publishable, and it provides a source of photography. All of that has become a wonderful enrichment that comes from my job. Because it's so close to what I would do if I just had the time to play, it blurs the line between vocation and avocation."

Do You Have What It Takes?

Rick Darke suggests that the following skills, in addition to a love of plants, are necessary for success in his profession:

"You need good writing skills and verbal communication. I could not do what I do, and I would not have had the opportunities if I hadn't worked on being able to articulate my notions."

Rick Darke's Background

Rick has a bachelor's degree in plant sciences from the University of Delaware. "I took a circuitous route. I spent seven years as an undergraduate and went through art and anthropology on the way to plant science. Longwood was my first job. I started as an intern there; then moved into an assistant taxonomist position. I did go back and take some graduate courses in plant systematics and taxonomy. However, instead of completing a graduate degree, it worked to my advantage to stay here. I ended up taking over a PhD position in taxonomy that was rewritten as a curator of plants. The man I was working for was due to retire in two years and it was a question of would I learn more by staying on the job and developing the skills I'd need to take over, or would I learn more by getting into a graduate program. My choice to stay worked out."

Anne Brennan, Student Intern

Anne Brennan graduated from Penn State with a BS in horticulture in December, 1993 and is working at Longwood Gardens doing a postgraduate internship in the education division. It's a 10-month paid internship that provides a monthly stipend of $800 and free housing. It also gives Anne a chance to experience different career options to help her decide what she would like to do.

Anne talks about her job and her future plans: "I started out thinking about horticultural production, growing the plants, as a possible career, whether in a greenhouse or nursery, but then I realized that there are so many more options out there. Here at Longwood Gardens I see new possibilities everyday.

"When I was in school I wasn't even aware that botanical gardens existed. Public gardens were not emphasized at my university. But they're very big, especially in the United States. There are botanical gardens everywhere and they all have horticulturists, they all have education people, publicists, and all different sorts of positions that are filled with people with horticultural backgrounds.

"I think I didn't know about it mainly because people teaching in universities have, of course, gone to graduate school and done research and that's what they see as horticulture—the academic and research end of things, or the production end of things. That's what direction a lot of them were pushed in, without even realizing it. My advisor kept mentioning grad school but I was never very excited about it, I didn't see how it would fit in for me. Now that I'm out of school and interacting with people who didn't all follow that path I see other options.

"My job here is unique because I work in the student programs office, which is the office that coordinates the internship program, as well as a two-year program called the professional gardener training program, and also an international student internship program with five students. So, I'm an intern coordinating other interns.

"It's very interesting. I'm working on a lot of different projects, a lot of day-to-day answering questions from people who are interested in the program. They call or write letters requesting information and I answer their requests.

"I'm also working on rewriting the promotional material on the three internship programs, and I organize the orientation program for the new interns. I arrange for different people to speak to the students, I give them a tour of the grounds, and organize field trips to other botanical gardens.

"My job involves a lot of communication skills. There are 40 students altogether in all different areas of the gardens. We have meetings twice a month and I write a long newsletter-type memo each week which includes things they need to know such as upcoming field trips.

"I like getting to meet all the new people who come in—I'm the first person they see when they arrive.

"I think I'm learning a lot of management skills, too. I have to run meetings; being in charge is not always comfortable for me but I'm getting used to it.

"I'm not exactly sure what I want to do when my internship is over. I am interested in garden writing. I've had a little experience working for a horticultural trade magazine and I did enjoy that. I don't know much about layout or publishing but I'm eager to learn.

"And I really enjoy what I'm doing here working in the education program of a public garden. That's also something I'd like to pursue as a full-time career.

"It would be nice to be able to land in a job as soon as I leave here but it probably won't happen that way. The job I'm doing now is strictly an intern position, so unless something else opens up, I'll have to move on."

The Arnold Arboretum

The Arnold Arboretum is located in Jamaica Plain, Massachusetts, a section of Boston, and is affiliated with Harvard University. Its mission is the biology, cultivation, and conservation of temperate woody plants. Within that mission falls the goals of continuing research, education, and community outreach work.

The Arnold Arboretum was the brainchild of Harvard botanist Asa Gray. With a bequeath from James Arnold of New Bedford and help from the will's trustees, Gray was able to realize his dream.

The Arnold Arboretum started with 123 species of neglected woody plants in 1874 and has since grown to 265 beautifully maintained acres, with approximately 15,000 plants in its living collection.

An Outreach Horticulturist at the Arnold Arboretum

Chris Strand is an outreach horticulturist at the Arnold Arboretum. He earned his BA in biology from the University of

Colorado in Boulder in 1989, focusing on taxonomy, the study of the different species and how they are classified.

After he graduated he won a fellowship sponsored by Longwood Gardens and earned his master's degree in public horticulture at the University of Delaware, in Newark. He worked for one year at Callaway Gardens near Atlanta, Georgia; then started with the Arnold Arboretum in 1993.

Chris talks about his job: "I'm in charge of visitor services and under that I have a wide range of duties. I develop and manage the exhibits that go in our exhibit hall. That's where all the information is disseminated to visitors. It's small, the real exhibit is the 265 acres of grounds that make up the arboretum, but in the exhibit hall we have an information desk and photographs and a bookstore with books on woody plants for sale.

"I have to make sure there are volunteers stationed in the exhibit hall to answer visitors' questions, and I train the volunteers so they know how to answer the questions.

"I make sure the bookstore buyer has everything she needs; I make sure there are maps of the grounds available so that people can navigate around the landscape. I put together lists of what's in flower and post upcoming events.

"On a typical day I make sure the exhibit hall is in shape and then I work on any number of projects. Right now I'm involved with putting together a map of the great trees of the arboretum. We have about 15,000 and I choose a few that people would be interested in seeing and put them in a brochure. I also coordinate the volunteers and I have a couple of high school students who are helping with the project.

"On any given day I also teach classes; I'm an instructor in the adult education program. I cover woody plant identification and I teach a six-week course on the highlights of the arboretum. My students are interested in continuing education; they are retired people, volunteers wanting to learn more about the plants, or rangers from the National Park Service.

"We have a cooperative arrangement with the National Park Service. Interpretative rangers used to be stationed here to conduct tours on the historical design of the landscape. Now we're teaching them how to do historical landscape restoration and maintenance. We deal mostly with woody plants and how to replace one as it grows older, maintaining the spirit of the landscape.

"I'm also working on ground signage. Right now there's nothing on the grounds to direct people except for two "You Are Here" maps. It's been an ongoing project. We have a consultant I work with on that.

"I also answer requests for information on the Arboretum and requests for publications. I have volunteers who run a plant answer line once a week so I supply them with all the books they need. They answer probably 40 questions a day during the spring.

"But best of all, I get to spend a lot of time out in the collections. My boss has made it clear that I'm supposed to be very familiar with everything, so I spend a lot of time going outside looking at plants, photographing them, learning about them. We have well over 11,000 different specimens on the grounds and the best part is that I always have the opportunity to learn more about them.

"The worst part is dealing with some difficult people. We are a public park and we don't charge admission. Some people disregard the rules. For example, they bring their dogs in and don't clean up after them or don't keep them leashed. We had a family of goslings but there's only one left now because the retrievers fetch them.

"There have been people who have vandalized the property or who have clipped all the peonies to sell on the street corner. The Boston park rangers patrol the grounds but they can't be everywhere at once."

Climbing the Career Ladder in Public Horticulture

Graduate programs in public horticulture are directed toward people who are interested in working in education or administration.

Chris Strand tells us his future career plans: "I think I'll continue to work in some sort of public program. Eventually I'd like to be in charge of a public program at an arboretum or botanic garden, moving up the ladder on the same track I'm on now.

"But I hope I'll always be able to have contact with the plants because that's the best part of the job. The more administrative your position, the less contact you have."

Mapping and Labeling

Susan Kelley is a curatorial associate for the living collections at Arnold Arboretum. Her job involves mapping the living specimens on the grounds and labeling each plant.

Susan talks about her job: "We're more than a horticultural garden. Our collections are used scientifically. We have a lot of visitors from all over the world who use our collections for study. Maps showing where each individual plant is on the grounds have been kept since the 1930s.

"Right now we're in the process of switching over from a series of about 100 hand-drawn maps to a computerized mapping system using a computer-aided design system. We're honing down to about 65 maps plus insets. My job is not only to transcribe the hand-drawn maps to the computerized, but also to maintain current hand-drawn maps in the interim. We have two major plantings a year, in the spring and in the fall, and probably 1,000 new plants go out every year onto the grounds. My job is to put the new plantings on the maps.

"I also field check each individual specimen for condition. If it's damaged I let the propagator know it might need to be repropagated. I recommend to the horticultural taxonomist or the superintendent of the grounds if something needs to be removed. The plant could be dying, diseased, or suffering damage from the weather or vandalism.

"I'm also responsible for making sure that every plant is labeled. The labels are hung directly on the plant. Each plant is supposed to have two records labels which give an accession number, the name of the plant, the family, where it came from, and the map location.

"When a plant goes from the nursery to the grounds is when I take over and maintain the records on each plant. We have about 15,000 on the grounds now. My boss is the horticultural taxonomist and we work very closely together. He decides what goes out on the grounds every spring and fall, assessing what's in the nursery and what will be planted. He puts together the planting bulletins, which are then handed to me. I use those to map the new plantings.

"And I'm supposed to be able to identify everything. Labels do get lost sometimes, or switched by the public. If there are any problems and I can't figure out what a plant is, for example, I ask him. There are specific plant families he's interested in and people from all over the world send him things to identify.

"The labels I'm responsible for are the size of a credit card and are made out of anodized aluminum. We gather the information on the plant from our computer's data base and lay it out with the correct number of lines and spaces. We have an embossing machine that actually prints out the label.

"Seventy percent of my time is spent outdoors, even in the winter. I have a lot of mapping and record keeping to do then. It's a great time to field check the conifer collection, the pines, the firs, the spruce, etc. You can also find labels more easily when there aren't any leaves on the trees, because they're hung above the ground level. With shrubs, though, it's a disaster to find the labels when there's snow on the ground."

How Susan Got Started

Susan started out as a violinist and earned both a bachelor's and master's degree in music before she decided to switch careers.

"I was freelancing in New York and it was a difficult life. I had plenty of work but everyone was so unhappy living there. Plants had always been an interest of mine growing up in Tennessee and I loved gardening.

"I went back to school to City University of New York and got my MA in plant population ecology.

"I worked at the Harvard University Herbaria in Cambridge for awhile as a partial employee of Arnold Arboretum. So naturally I met people from the Arnold Arboretum; they would come to Cambridge, I would go to Jamaica Plain. When my current position became available I applied. I prefer being outdoors as opposed to working indoors all day.

"Because of the relationship of Harvard and the Arboretum we are all technically employees of Harvard—and we get all the benefits of a Harvard employee. We can take courses for $40, there are excellent health benefits, life insurance, and a free pass to all the museums in Boston and the surrounding area."

The Pluses and Minuses of Susan's Job

"What I love most is being outdoors in this great collection of plants. It's one of the best collections in the world. There are very old specimens and then we have all these new plants coming in. I also like that I have some indoor work. The computer work I do is challenging mentally. The mix is ideal.

"The only stress I have is that we're understaffed and my job is extensive enough that three people should really be doing it. I do have volunteers I coordinate and I have two interns in the summertime who help. But managing people can also add to the stress. You have to take the time to train them and it's extra work. We get applicants from all over the world for the internship program here and we don't interview in person. It's always tricky to interview someone over the phone and try to get an idea how they would work out.

"But whenever I need to regroup I can just go outside. I have a beautiful place in which to do it."

The Career Ladder for Mappers and Labelers

Susan discusses the options: "This is a great job, I could feasibly stay here for a long time. There's so much more to learn. For example, there's another mapping system I'm interested in— GIS, Geographic Information System.

"With more experience, more study and research and publications, one could move up into a curatorial position. I'd want to become more proficient with taxonomic work and go on collecting trips. We have a research program in Indonesia and I'd love to go there one day and do mapping at their botanical gardens."

Internships at Botanical Gardens and Arboreta

"Horticulture is an occupation you can't learn by just being in the classroom," says Dave Foresman, student programs coordinator at Longwood Gardens. "You have to have work experience and on-the-job training. We would not hire anybody without work experience, whether it's summer work or a bona fide internship program. This is very important."

Most public gardens offer some sort of student internship program, though they might differ in the degree of responsibility the intern has and the departments in which she could be placed.

"Longwood's internships differ quite a bit from other botanical gardens," Dave explains. "We're providing gardening experience. We have people in other divisions, but most of our interns our working either outside in the gardens or in the conservatories doing the same kind of work our gardeners are doing each day. They're learning those skills, the equipment, methods, and procedures used in public display facilities.

"In other gardens internships might provide more responsibility. A student could be rotated throughout various work areas. Our interns apply and are chosen for a specific location. For example, if they elect a flower garden internship, they will stay in that division throughout their internship. There might be eight to ten stations you might work at in the flower garden but you wouldn't normally come in and work in the greenhouse or in research.

"You can't become a botanist or curator without becoming a gardener first. You have to know the basic techniques."

Internships can run from three months to a year. Usually interns are in their junior or senior year of college or are recent graduates. Interns work from 35 to 40 hours per week and can be placed in any department within the botanical garden or arboretum.

Some gardens offer Professional Gardener programs. Longwood's program is a two-year stint combining academics and hands-on training.

Dave Foresman explains Longwood Gardens' Professional Gardener program. "Students in this program move around to different departments on a scheduled rotation. These are paid positions with housing. Students spend 10 hours a week in the classroom for a two-year period and 25 hours a week receiving hands-on training.

"Graduates from our Professional Gardener program are very much sought after. The program is twenty-four years old and we've had only 137 graduates in that time. Just this morning we had two job offerings that came in by phone. We post 50 to 75 jobs a year and we graduate only about 14 students every other year."

Internships at some gardens are very competitive. Longwood has only 40 slots for their student internship program but they receive 120 applications a year.

To find the internship or professional gardener program that's right for you, you can contact the garden of your choice directly or go through your university department's internship office.

There is also a directory of more than 500 internships and summer programs published by the American Association of Botanical Gardens and Arboreta (AABGA). Their address is given at the end of this chapter.

The addresses of selected botanical gardens and arboreta are listed in Appendix A.

Arboriculture

Arboriculture is defined as the preservation and care of trees and shrubs, and can include woody vines as well as ground cover plantings.

Arborists are the tree experts who take care of the trees. They have many responsibilities including planting and transplanting trees, pruning and trimming them, spraying for insects, treating for diseases, fertilizing, bracing, installing lightening protection, and when necessary, removing them.

Professional arborists also work as consultants. They provide inspections of trees and landscape plants and make reports to insurance companies on tree and other landscape loss due to storm damage, automobile accidents, or vandalism. They can also act as expert witnesses, providing testimony in court cases.

Consulting arborists are qualified to establish dollar values for trees for the purpose of real estate appraisals. During construction of new property, arborists assist in the preservation of existing trees, prepare specifications for the planting of new trees, and diagnose any problems.

The Work Involved

For the most part, hands-on tree workers perform jobs that require a great deal of physical labor. They climb trees or work from an aerial lift or a cherry picker, a truck-mounted crane with a large bucket on the end in which the worker stands.

They handle heavy and dangerous equipment, such as chain saws, hydraulic pruners, and stump grinders. They work from great heights, and haul branches and other cumbersome material. Arborists also handle pesticides and chemicals for preventative and corrective measures in the treatment of insect problems or diseases. To apply these pesticides, they must be licensed and follow state and federal laws regulating the use of chemicals.

Job Settings for Arborists

Arborists can work almost anywhere in the country. Power companies hire tree workers to clear tree growth from telephone and power lines. City and county highway departments employ tree experts to plant and care for trees and shrubs along roadsides. Public parks require the services of arborists to maintain healthy trees in recreation areas. Arboreta employ professional arborists to care for their living collections. Private homeowners, condominium complexes, and shopping centers use arborists to plant or remove trees and to treat them for any diseases or insect problems. Landscape contractors also utilize the services of professional arborists.

Training and Qualifications for Tree Workers

Requirements vary, but helpers, ground workers, and climbers seldom need a formal education. However, high school is desirable. For those who will advance, a knowledge of the following disciplines is necessary: arboriculture, biology, botany, entomology, and plant pathology.

Vocational schools and two-year community colleges offer training in this increasingly complex work. On-the-job training is equally important.

To use pesticides, a tree worker must be licensed by a state environmental department. It is also necessary to have a driver's license, preferably a commercial license for driving trucks and tractors.

The International Society of Arboriculture grants prestigious certification to arborists with experience and education who pass a comprehensive written examination.

Salaries for Arborists

Just as the duties of arborists vary, so do salaries. Physical laborers, who generally work the hardest, are paid from $12,000 to $20,000 per year for ground work, from $15,000 to $30,000 for climbing. Supervisors or consulting arborists, who rely more on their years of experience and expertise than physical strength, can be paid $35,000 and up.

Job Outlook

Tree care is a promising field. There is a shortage of arborists, possibly because of the low pay and hard work for starting workers.

But more and more homeowners, businesses, and cities and towns are recognizing the importance of trees to the environment. A growing commitment to historic preservation and environmental planning also is improving the job market.

A Self-Employed Arborist

Way Hoyt is owner of Tree Trimmers and Associates, Inc. "The trees are our associates," Way says. "They have a big part in our business."

Way's wife, Geri Hoyt, is the owner of Arborist Supply House, which sells ropes, saddles, pruners, shears, and other equipment for tree workers.

Way Hoyt has been planting trees ever since he was about seven years old. "I'm the little kid who ran along the turnpike taking Australian Pine saplings out, then transplanting them in my yard. I didn't get in trouble with my folks for doing that until the trees grew to be humongous."

Way has an associate's degree and attended the University of Florida at the research and experimental station in Ft. Lauderdale. He has been in business 18 years.

"I chose self-employment first for financial reasons. But when I was working for other companies I found out that they were basically doing terrible things to the trees. I went into my own business so I could do proper tree trimming.

"Pruning done correctly is the healthiest thing a tree can have done to it. Done incorrectly, as in stubs, nubs, rips, tears, flesh cuts, too much green being removed, or not enough attention paid to structural material, can be the worst treatment done to the tree."

One of Way's concerns about the profession is the abundance of what he calls hat rack specialists. "This is a term used for mutilating trees, and that's what an awful lot of tree services continue to do. There are right ways and wrong ways of treating trees and there is a world of information on tree trimming, but it's been my experience that a large percentage of tree trimmers don't know anything about it. Anybody who can work a chain saw thinks he can trim a tree and anybody can hang out a shingle and call themselves an arborist, even if they're not. All that is required is a small fee to the county for an occupational license and then you can legally call yourself a tree expert."

Way is also concerned about conservation. His company motto is "a tree company with our environment and associated ecology, performing tree work both scientifically and aesthetically."

Way encourages people to attend good programs and get the proper training. He also teaches courses at Flamingo Gardens on arboriculture, tree identification, and what happens inside a tree when it's been damaged on the outside.

In addition, he has been asked on numerous occasions to appear as an expert witness in court. He talks about his most recent case:

"A fellow was driving east during story weather along a four-lane highway with a median strip. The trunk of a black olive tree split and fell on his car as he was driving by at about 45 to 50 miles per hour. He was seriously injured, permanently paralyzed in fact.

"A few months before the accident the tree had been trimmed. I took a look at the tree and saw indications of serious structural problems. The trimming done was not adequate. They should have notified the property owner of a possible dangerous situation, but they didn't. The professional maintenance company and the condominium complex that own the tree are being sued.

"When I go into court, I'll talk about the tree and the structure and that it was an accident waiting to happen."

Summing up his feelings about his profession, Way says, "You can certainly make a career out of it and never stop learning.

And it's very satisfying. You can step back and look at what you have accomplished and know that you did a nice job, helping a tree."

Further Reading

The following resources are publications of the American Association of Botanical Gardens and Arboreta (AABGA) and can be ordered directly from them at their address below.

Salary Survey Contains the latest salary and benefit information for 22 positions in administration, horticulture, and education at U.S. and Canadian botanical gardens.

Internship Directory Lists over 500 summer jobs and internships at 125 botanical gardens, arboreta, and other horticultural institutions. Includes positions in grounds management, education, collections, curation, and more.

A Directory of Volunteer Programs at Public Gardens The directory profiles 121 volunteer programs at public gardens, listing volunteer services, special events, and the addresses and telephone numbers for volunteer coordinators.

For Further Information

American Association of Botanical
Gardens and Arboreta (AABGA)
786 Church Rd.
Wayne, PA 19087

American Society of Consulting Arborists
5130 W. 101st Circle
Westminster, CO 80030

Arnold Arboretum
125 Arbor Way
Jamaica Plain, MA 02130
Attn: Internship Coordinator

International Society of Arboriculture
P.O. Box GG
Savoy, IL 61874

Longwood Gardens
P.O. Box 501
Kennett Square, PA 19348
Attn: Student Programs Coordinator

National Arbor Day Foundation/Institute
100 Arbor Ave.
Nebraska City, NE 68410

National Arborist Association
P.O. Box 1094
Amherst, NH 03031-1094
Offers training programs for arborists.

Plant Scientists and Educators

The scientific study of plants encompasses a wide range of focuses and careers and covers the biological as well as agricultural sciences. Plant lovers choosing to become scientists can work with soil and crops, researching ways to improve food production. They can use their knowledge to battle insects or disease by producing environmentally sound pesticides or herbicides. Plant scientists also can teach and train future plant scientists and other horticultural professionals.

Plant lovers in the education field work with the general public as well as student horticulturalists. They provide information in botanic gardens and arboreta (see Chapter Four for careers in those settings) and also through nurseries and the Cooperative Extension Service.

Job settings are as varied as the work. A plant scientist could be employed on a working or experimental farm, in a botanical garden, in a government or private research laboratory, in a school or university classroom, or aboard a ship.

Educators also have varied settings including public gardens, research facilities, private nurseries, and universities and adult education programs throughout the country.

Plant scientists work indoors with computers, microscopes, and electronic instruments or outside with their hands, collecting soil and plant samples. They can even work underwater, gathering specimens from the ocean floor.

Educators work in the field or in the classroom. They teach theory or practical hands-on methods. They answer questions, offer suggestions, and help the public with a variety of plant and ecological issues.

In general, scientists working with plants study their various properties, the conditions under which they grow best, and their relationship with the environment. They identify and classify them, protect them from pests and disease, and conduct research to develop better crop yields or new medicines.

In this chapter you will find a definition of each science and the working conditions, training levels required, and approximate salaries. You will also learn about different research facilities as well as the Cooperative Extension Service and the important work they do in almost every U.S. community.

Careers in the Plant Sciences

As the world grows more and more complex we are continually faced with more and more complex environmental concerns—a declining biological diversity and the need for increased food production. And these are just some of the problems addressed by plant biology professionals.

Are You a Problem Solver?

Take this little quiz to see if you have the necessary interests to pursue a career in the plant sciences. Answer Yes or No.

Yes No

1. Are you fascinated by the wonders of the world? ___ ___
2. Do you find yourself often asking the question "Why?" ___ ___
3. Are you a collector? (Stamps, coins, rocks, etc.?) ___ ___
4. Do you enjoy solving puzzles? ___ ___
5. Have you ever thought of a method to answer a question you or someone else might have posed? ___ ___
6. Is it important to you to help the world in a meaningful way? ___ ___

If you answered "Yes" to any of these questions, you already share some of the characteristics of plant scientists. Let's find out what biologists do and how you might fit in.

What Is Botany?

In its broadest sense, botany is the study of plants, from the smallest microscopic organism to giant sequoia trees. Because the field is so broad, there are many different kinds of plant biologists. Just as medicine has specialties—surgery, internal medicine, and dermatology, for example—within botany there are many subspecialties.

The results of botanical research are to increase and improve medicines, foods, fibers, building materials, and other plant products. Plant scientists also help to solve our environmental problems.

What Plant Scientists Do

One of the most attractive features of the field of plant science is the number of different specialties and options from which a plant lover can choose. Look at the chart below and find the interest area or background skills you possess. By scanning across the chart you can find the specialty that might be right for you.

INTEREST/SKILL	SPECIALTY
Mathematics	Biophysics
	Genetics
	Systems ecology
Outdoor activities	Ecology
	Forestry
	Phycology
	Plant exploration
	Taxonomy
Chemistry	Chemotaxonomy
	Molecular biology
	Plant biochemistry
	Plant physiology
Intricate forms and designs	Plant structure—cytology, anatomy, and morphology

INTEREST/SKILL	SPECIALTY
Organisms not visible to the naked eye	Brycology Microbiology Mycology Phycology
World food supply	Agronomy Food science Plant breeding Plant pathology
History and Evolution	Morphology Paleobotany
Working with people	Education Public Service Teaching

The Specialties

You've looked down the chart and found your interests—but what are all those specialized fields across the chart about? Here is a brief description (in alphabetical order) of many of the different scientific specialties:

Agronomy Agronomists make practical use of plant and soil sciences to increase the yield of crops.

Anatomy The study of plant cells and tissues.

Biochemistry The study of the chemical aspects of plant life processes, including the chemical products of plants (phytochemistry).

Biophysics The application of physics to plant life processes.

Breeding Selecting and crossing plants with desirable traits to develop plants that are more useful to humans such as those that would be resistant to diseases.

Brycology The study of mosses and similar plants, including their identification, classification, and ecology.

Chemotaxonomy Using the chemicals produced by plant groups to aid in their identification.

Cytology The study of plant cell structure, function, and life history.

Ecology The relationships between plants and the world in which they live.

Food science The development of food from various plant products.

Forestry Forest management for conservation and the production of timber.

Genetics The study of plant heredity, genes, and gene function.

Microbiology The study of microorganisms.

Molecular biology The study of the structure and function of biological macromolecules.

Morphology The study of the evolution and development of leaves, roots, and stems.

Mycology The biology of fungi.

Paleobotany The study of the biology and evolution of fossil plants.

Pathology The study of the origins and management of plant diseases.

Phycology The study of algae. Phycologists who study algae in oceans are sometimes also called marine biologists.

Physiology The study of the functions and life processes of plants such as photosynthesis and mineral nutrition.

Plant exploration The search for new, undiscovered plants.

Taxonomy The identification and classification of plants.

Employment for Plant Scientists

Most plant biologists are employed by educational institutions, federal and state agencies, and private industries.

At educational institutions plant scientists teach, conduct research, or perform a combination of the two activities.

Within the government plant scientists can work in a number of different settings. They are employed by the U.S. Department of Agriculture, which includes the U.S. Forest Service; the U.S. Department of the Interior, which includes the National Park Service (for information on the National Park Service see Chapter Three) and the U.S. Geological Survey; the Public Health Service; the State Department; the Smithsonian Institution; and the Environmental Protection Agency.

Within the private sector, plant scientists are employed by pharmaceutical companies, the petrochemical industry, the chemical industry, lumber and paper industries, nurseries, food growers, breweries, and biotechnical firms.

Qualifications

Four years of college and a bachelor's degree are the minimum requirements for most positions. A bachelor's level scientist can work as a laboratory technician or a technical assistant in educational institutions, industry, government, museums, and botanical gardens.

A wider range of positions is available for those who have worked toward higher degrees. Most teaching and research positions at the university level require a doctorate degree.

Getting a Head Start

High school students can prepare themselves by concentrating on the sciences, mathematics, English, and history. Participation in science fairs and science clubs can also provide valuable experience, as would summer employment in biology related fields.

Education

Educators play an important role in the world of plant science. The information that researchers and scientists uncover is not worth much if it can't be shared. Only by sharing knowledge can people be made aware of world problems. And awareness is the first step toward solving problems.

There are many environments in addition to the traditional university setting in which a dedicated plant lover can share information. Education positions within botanical gardens and arboreta are explored in Chapter Four. The remainder of this chapter introduces you to the Cooperative Extension Service and two research centers dedicated to promoting awareness of different earth problems.

Read on to see if a career in plant education would be right for you.

The Cooperative Extension Service

In the early 1900s the United States was largely an agrarian society. The farmers felt they needed more information about agriculture in order to do a better job feeding the nation. At that time approximately 40 percent of the population was spread out in rural areas, and the rest resided in urban centers. Now the proportions have changed, with only about 3 or 4 percent living in agricultural areas and rural settings.

There were a number of issues that were brought before Congress at the time to help the nation's agricultural interests. First, a bill was passed forming land-grant colleges so that every state would have a college that would be technical in nature with its main focus to conduct research in agriculture.

Second, Congress recognized the need for physical locations in which to conduct related research. Because of the type of research needed, it couldn't be done in a laboratory, it had to be done out in the field. This brought about the establishment of research stations associated with each land-grant college. They were located at the universities, or nearby, wherever the crops were. In some states more than one research station was set up.

Third, it was realized that with all this new research and knowledge being gained, there needed to be a way to disseminate the information. This is how the Cooperative Extension Service was born.

The title "Cooperative" was chosen because the program is funded with state, county, and federal monies. Every county has at least one, if not more, programs. There is an advisory board for each county that points out areas that need to be addressed and services that need to be offered.

What the Cooperative Extension Service Does

The function of the Cooperative Extension Service has expanded beyond agricultural issues and now also covers home economics, the 4-H youth program, and a program that helps commercial fisherman.

The Cooperative Extension Service works with the community and tries to bring the research that is done at the universities out to the public where it's needed. To do this, the Cooperative Extension Service employs professional horticulturists and educators in the job title of Cooperative Extension Agent.

An Agent with the Cooperative Extension Service

Loretta Hodyss has been a Cooperative Extension Agent in Palm Beach County, Florida since 1979. "In a county like Palm Beach with a population of 900,000, maybe only 10,000 are associated with agriculture and the rest are urban. Therefore, the largest component of our work is urban horticulture. We answer people's questions about their lawns or how to grow a certain plant on the window sill or how to grow vegetables, trees, shrubs. Whatever is needed. The service is free to the public, but we have to charge for some publications and classes to cover expenses."

Loretta works mainly with the county's commercial nursery industry. "I spend my time answering questions, helping them with their crop problems—mostly insect and disease related issues. In Palm Beach County it's a $200,000,000 industry. We have 600 nurseries, which keep me pretty busy.

"Some of my work I do over the telephone. We're open for questions from the public from 9 A.M. to 5 P.M. Monday through Friday. And although we can't do this for homeowners, very frequently I will go out to the nurseries to answer questions.

"We also have a lot of educational programs, all different sorts of classes, newsletters we send out, and published material we distribute. Whatever technical mechanism we can use to get the information out we do it."

Loretta likes having a challenging job with something different to do every day. "There's always something new and interesting to learn and you're constantly encouraged to go back to school and learn. There is a wealth of information out there—and a wealth of people who are appreciative of your help.

"My role is that of educator more than anything else. Many of us do research also. We've struggled with the title; we'd rather be called Extension Educators than Extension Agents, and in some states they have changed it."

Becoming a Cooperative Extension Agent

An Extension Agent is an employee of the land-grant college and the county. The position requires a master's degree in whatever field is appropriate—vegetable science, entomology, pathology, or any related subjects. Loretta Hodyss has a master's in horticulture.

"There is a growing need for policy-making agents," Loretta explains, "people who will work with the community on environmental issues. These agents could be sociologists, for example. We're all called Extension Agents but the job can cover a lot of different specialties.

"What we do is determined by the needs of the county. If they were growing cotton here I'd have to be a cotton specialist. If we had cows I'd need a vet/med background."

The number of agents varies with the county. In Loretta's office there are 12 agents. Five deal with home economics, and the youth and fishermen programs; seven cover urban and agricultural horticulture.

"In some counties in Florida, there are affiliated positions that are called County Agents. The titles vary from state to state, but in Florida a county agent is employed solely by the county. That position doesn't require a master's, but it does require a bachelor's."

Every office also has a director to whom the Extension Agents report. To become a director, a master's degree is required as well as several years of experience working as an Extension Agent.

And the willingness to work hard is also a requirement. Loretta explains: "You're on call 24 hours. Some of us carry beepers. I have a cellular phone that's always with me. That can be troublesome. If there's a hurricane or heavy rain or some disaster, we are expected to help and answer questions about what people should do in those situations. People rely on us heavily. That's what we want, but for some people it can be stressful.

"I find it gratifying, though. You need to be the kind of person who can deal with that."

Salaries for Extension Agents

Salaries follow state and county scales and vary from region to region. A bachelor's level affiliated agent could expect to earn in the high teens. A new agent just out of graduate school could expect to earn $20,000 to $25,000 a year.

After a few years of experience, salaries increase with cost of living and merit raises.

Finding a Job with the Cooperative Extension Service

Although the Cooperative Extension Service has a national office in Washington, D.C., there is no national job bank. Positions are usually posted at the land-grant colleges, and the individual county offices are then notified.

Contacting the state university is the best place to start. You can find your local Extension Office in the telephone book under county or state government offices.

For those wishing a career with the Cooperative Extension Service, it's a good idea to be prepared to relocate. You can decide upon an area of the country in which you would like to work, making sure you are familiar with the different horticultural requirements of that area. Then call the various land-grant colleges for job openings.

National Wildflower Research Center

The National Wildflower Research Center is the only national nonprofit research and educational organization committed to the preservation of native plants in planned landscapes. Founded in 1982 by Lady Bird Johnson, the Wildflower Center recently moved from its location in a former hayfield east of Austin, Texas to a new facility with 34,000 square feet of buildings and 72,000 square feet of display gardens and educational demonstration areas. They now have 42 acres of Texas hill country southwest of Austin in which to conduct educational programs and research.

The Wildflower Center is dedicated exclusively to the study, preservation, and re-establishment of native plants in public and private landscapes. The Wildflower Center strives to restore damaged habitats by sharing its knowledge and encouraging state highway departments, landscape architects and designers, developers, teachers, and backyard gardeners to use native plants.

These are some of the National Wildflower Research Center's special facilities:

Children's garden

Meditation garden

Observation tower

Rainwater collection and harvesting system

Research laboratory

Seed silo

Theme gardens

Three greenhouses

Three home-comparison gardens

Volunteer workroom

Staffing at The National Wildflower Research Center
At present the Wildflower Center employs the following professionals:

Bookkeeper

Botanists (2)

Development associate

Development director

Editor

Education director

Executive director

Facility sales manager

Horticulturist

Landscape manager

Products manager

Public relations and marketing manager

Records/membership manager

Support staff (2–3)

Because the Wildflower Center is nonprofit and privately funded, it relies heavily on the help of more than 200 volunteers. Activities range from hosting fundraisers to designing curriculum for science teachers. Volunteering at this center and others like it is an excellent way for plant lovers to acquire some practical hands-on training in a number of different disciplines. For more information contact: The National Wildflower Research Center, 2600 FM 973 North, Austin, TX 78725-4201.

World Forestry Center

The World Forestry Center was built in 1905 as the "Forestry Center" for the Lewis and Clark Exposition held in Portland, Oregon. Its beautiful log cabin and all of its contents were destroyed by fire in 1964. The "Western Forestry Center" was reconstructed in 1971 and renamed the "World Forestry Center" in 1986.

The World Forestry Center is an educational organization aiming to increase understanding of the importance of well-managed forests and their related resources. Through its publications, educational programs, exhibits, and architecture, the Center demonstrates the benefits of conserving the forest environment.

The World Forestry Center is also dedicated to the conservation of soil, trees, wildlife, water, and other natural resources. It accomplishes its mission through scientific research, demonstrations, and the distribution of forestry information. For more information about all the varied programs and volunteering opportunities contact World Forestry Center, 4033 SW Canyon Rd., Portland, OR 97221.

For more information about careers in forestry, see Chapter Three.

Further Reading

Guide to Graduate Study in Botany is for any graduate student contemplating a career in plant biology. It lists the plant science departments in the United States and Canada that offer a PhD degree in some area of the plant sciences. Each listing includes information about the department and its faculty. The guide is available from: Manager of Publications, Botanical Society of America, Department of Botany, Ohio State University, 1735 Neil Avenue, Columbus, OH 43210.

For Further Information

American Institute of Biological Sciences
730 11th St., N.W.
Washington, D.C. 20001-4584

American Society of Agronomy
677 South Segoe Rd.
Madison, WI 53711

American Society of Plant Taxonomists
c/o Rancho Santa Ana Botanic Garden
1500 North College Ave.
Claremont, CA 91711

Botanical Society of America
Department of Botany
Ohio State University
1735 Neil Ave.
Columbus, OH 43210

Cooperative Extension Service
National Office
USDA; ES
14th St. and Independence Ave.
Washington, D.C. 20250

National Wildflower Research Center
2600 FM 973 North
Austin, TX 78725-4201

Office of Opportunities in Sciences
1776 Massachusetts Ave., N.W.
Washington, D.C. 20036

Organization of Biological Field Stations
Tyson Research Center
P.O. Box 258
Eureka, MO 63025

Sea Education Association
P.O. Box 6
Woods Hole, MA 02543

Soil Conservation Service
14th St. and Independence Ave., S.W.
Washington, D.C. 20013

Soil Science Society of America
677 South Segoe Rd.
Madison, WI 53711

U.S. Environmental Protection Agency
Personnel Management Division (PM-212)
Washington, D.C. 20460

CHAPTER SIX

Healing with Plants

For thousands of years people have recognized the healing properties of plants. Before the creation of synthetic medicines, ancient cultures were knowledgeable about each plant's function and how to tap into its strengths.

In modern times in the United States, this discipline has become almost a lost art. But not quite. Plant lovers around the world still recognize the value of plants for healing.

In addition to their aesthetic value and life-sustaining importance as food, plants have always been the basis for curing common and not so common ailments. Products derived from plants provide us with therapeutic and curative powers.

Plant lovers with a healing nature can find rewarding careers in this area.

Herbalism

Old Webster's Dictionary from the 1800s defined an herbalist as one involved with the commerce of plants—an herb doctor or root doctor. Today, most people refer to herbalists as those who use or pick herbs for medicine.

Herbalists fall into several different categories. Wildcrafters are herbalists who pick herbs to be used for medicinal purposes. Farmers who specifically grow herbs for medicine are considered to be herbalists. People who make products out of herbs such as potpourris and wreaths (see the section under "Craftspeople" in Chapter Two), or herbal manufacturers, can also be called herbalists. Herbologists, as the suffix implies, are people who study herbs and identify them—but don't necessarily use them.

The Birth of an Herbalist

Roy Upton, president of the American Herbalist Guild, is an herbalist who, through his writing and lecturing, is involved with teaching people the medicinal value of plants. He writes books and magazine articles and teaches classes across the country. He is very knowledgeable about people's health needs and which types of herbs can be used to deal with different types of ailments. In addition, Roy works full-time for a manufacturer of medicinal products, responsible for quality control and answering customers' questions.

Roy Upton came across his expertise in an interesting manner. He lived for three and half years on different Native American reservations, in Washington, Nevada, and New Mexico, learning about herbs and their uses. "I just learned about herbs as a process of living," explains Roy. "People got sick, the medicine people picked herbs and made teas or poultices. I absorbed what I was seeing and started learning."

He then spent four years in St. Thomas, Virgin Islands, and studied the Caribbean's ethnobotany (how cultures use plants for medicine.) "There are different herb doctors in the Caribbean; people go to them just like they go to regular doctors here. One of my teachers was too old to gather the plants, so I would do it for her, and then she would tell me what they were used for. I would then comb through all the literature in the libraries, and eventually, while working on a project for the local college in St. Thomas, cataloging the different medicinal plants and setting up medicinal herb gardens, I learned even more."

From there Roy traveled to California, where he is currently based, and entered into a three-year program studying traditional Chinese medicine.

For those seeking training as an herbalist, and not able to follow in Roy's footsteps, there are a number of residency programs in the United States. There are also correspondence courses and various lectures, seminars, and workshops held across the country. The American Herbalist Guild publishes an inexpensive directory that lists all the different programs. It is available by writing to them at their address listed at the end of this chapter.

The Politics of Herbalism

Although herbalism has been practiced pretty much in the same manner for thousands of years, finding recognition through established channels in this country could take another millennium or two, U.S. herbalists believe.

Roy Upton says, "There is a monopolistic control of health care in this country. Things like midwifery, which is accepted worldwide, or herbalism, which is also accepted worldwide by other cultures, are not warmly embraced in this country. But that's changing.

"Presently, there are only two mechanisms by which someone can be licensed to practice medicine and utilize herbs in his or her practice. The first is to become licensed as a naturopathic physician. Naturopathic physicians are fully trained through medical schools and are called ND's, as opposed to MD's. Naturopathic medicine is essentially the practice of health by utilizing the principles of nature, such as diet, exercise, and herbal medicine.

"The other way to become licensed to use herbs is as an acupuncturist. Acupuncture is a foundation of Chinese medicine, and herbalism plays a large role in that discipline. But it has to be through a program that teaches herbal medicine. Not all acupuncture programs do."

What an Herbalist Does

Herbalists are familiar with the medicinal properties of various herbs and know which herbs can help with particular physical or emotional problems. However, unless they are licensed in either of the two above-mentioned categories, herbalists cannot hang out a shingle and practice medicine in this country, even if in that practice all they are doing is recommending herbal teas.

According to Roy Upton, "Under the FDA, the Federal Food and Drug Administration, you cannot legally dispense a substance for medicinal use unless that substance has been approved by the FDA. If you give garlic to someone, for example, and tell him or her that it can help lower cholesterol levels, you can be arrested for dispensing illicit drugs. Garlic.

"But we are pushing the system to change."

If you walk into any nutrition and health store you'll see rows of bottles and vials holding all the different herbs in their various forms. How do manufacturers and retailers buck the system? In essence, they are selling non-FDA-approved substances, which are therefore considered illegal.

The answer is simple. The products are not packaged as medicines; they are called "foods."

Trained herbalists know what to do with these "foods." They are aware of how the popular medications used in this country—aspirins and sedatives, for example—can be substituted safely with common plants.

"Aspirin was originally derived from a plant called meadowsweet," Roy explains. "The Latin name at that time was spirea, which is where the *spir* in *aspirin* came from. So, if someone has a headache, for example, we would use a natural source, a tea made with meadowsweet.

"With sedatives, there are more than a million prescriptions written for Valium every year, which involves a $65 doctor visit and a $30 prescription, not to mention all the harmful implications. Instead, we would start with using something as simple as chamomile tea, which is what Peter Rabbit's mother gave him. Chamomile is a flower which has essential oils. These oils have calming and sedative properties. There are a whole range of calming herbs that get progressively stronger—from chamomile to skullcap to valerian root."

Herbalists get their message across without resorting to breaking the law. They teach and write books and articles, they lecture and offer apprentice programs or they work for herbal product manufacturers.

Jobs with Herbal Product Manufacturers

There are several jobs within the herbal product manufacturing industry:

Researching and developing formulas and processing techniques.

Monitoring quality control by insuring that the plants being used are the right plants, that they are not contaminated and that they have the potency you want them to have.

Writing literature to describe the products.

Teaching classes to increase consumer awareness about the different products.

Pharmacognosy

Pharmacology is the study of medicinal actions of substances in general. Pharmacognosy is the study of medicinal actions of plants and other natural products. It doesn't cover, as herbalism does, the practice of herbal medicine or the picking of medicinal plants.

It is the job of pharmacognosy professionals to pick the product apart and study its constituents. Roy explains: "Native American herbalists, for example, might not know that a plant contains volatile oils, alkaloids, and polysaccharides. They don't care about that. They know how to use it, how it works, and that's what's important.

"A pharmacognosist would study those elements, though they wouldn't necessarily know how to use them. The end result of their study is to try to develop synthetic drugs from the natural substances.

"Like herbalism, pharmacognosy was sort of an endangered species. At one time, physicians were trained in botany because they needed to know where their medicines came from. But then there was the separation between pharmacy and medicine, and other subspecialties were created such as pharmacology and pharmacognosy, which kept on studying medicinal plants. As the chemical revolution took place in the 1800's, there was a big push to develop medicines as patentable substances in order to create a pharmaceutical industry. The craft of the herbalist and the pharmacognosist was less valued. Doctors no longer studied botany and the thrust was to synthesize medicinal plants so they could be standardized to a certain level of activity. The professions almost died. It's only been in the last twenty years that there's been a resurgence."

The University of Illinois has one of the best training programs in the country in pharmacognosy. It is offered through the School of Pharmacology.

Horticultural Therapy

Any gardener can tell you that being close to the soil, working with plants or just sitting in a fragrant and colorful spot has therapeutic value. Horticultural activity has been long known to relieve tension, improve our physical condition, and promote a sense of accomplishment, pride, and well-being.

The earliest physicians in ancient Egypt prescribed walks in the garden for their mentally ill patients. Signer of the Declaration of Independence, physician Benjamin Rush, encouraged his psychiatric patients to tend gardens. In 1879, Pennsylvania's Friends Asylum for the Insane (today renamed Friends Hospital) built the first known greenhouse for use with mentally ill patients. And after World War II, veterans' hospitals—with the help of scores of garden club volunteers—also promoted similar activity for their physically and emotionally disabled patients.

Today, horticultural therapy is an emerging science based on this time-tested art. In 1955, Michigan State University awarded the first undergraduate degree in horticultural therapy and in 1971, Kansas State University established the first graduate program in the field.

What Is Horticultural Therapy?

Horticultural therapists use activities involving plants and other natural materials to rehabilitate and/or improve a person's social, educational, psychological, and physical adjustment.

Therapists work with people who are physically or developmentally disabled, the elderly, drug and alcohol abusers, prisoners, and those who are socially or economically disadvantaged.

Charles A. Lewis of the Morton Arboretum says, "Plants possess life-enhancing qualities that encourage people to respond to them. In a judgmental world, plants are nonthreatening and nondiscriminating. They are living entities that respond directly to the care that is given them, not to the intellectual or physical capacities of the gardener. In short, they provide a benevolent setting in which a person can take the first steps toward confidence."

Horticultural therapists, in addition to utilizing standard gardening routines, also introduce alternative methods that are sensitive to the special needs of patients. This involves constructing raised beds and building wide paths and gently graded entrances accessible to wheelchairs. Tools are also adapted; short handles, for example, work best with wheelchair-bound individuals, long handles for those with weak backs.

Job Outlook

Because of the continued growth of horticultural therapy, the demand for trained therapists has continued to rise. Horticultural therapists find work in rehab hospitals, nursing homes, substance abuse treatment centers, prisons, botanical gardens, and through inner city programs.

Finding that Job

Kansas State University in Manhattan, Kansas maintains a job bank, and the American Horticultural Therapy Association (AHTA) lists any openings of which they are made aware.

Some positions find their way into the Help Wanted section of local newspapers, but most horticultural therapists learn about positions through word of mouth—or they create their own.

Often administrators at rehab centers and hospitals and other appropriate settings aren't aware of the benefits of a horticultural therapy program. Enterprising therapists with PR skills have learned how to convince administrators that their services are needed.

Many begin by volunteering their time, working with patients or clients at the hospitals or through a local botanical garden. That's how Nancy Stevenson got her start over 20 years ago.

What It's Like to Be a Horticultural Therapist

Nancy Stevenson has worked as a horticultural therapist for over 20 years. She earned a bachelor's degree in political science; then later went on for a master's in human services and became registered by the American Horticultural Therapy Association.

"I got interested in horticultural therapy back in the early 70s when it was still just a fledgling profession," Nancy explains. "The national organization, AHTA, was founded in 1973. At first I was a volunteer at a boys' detention center, working with someone who had started an indoor gardening program there. My colleague, Libby Reavis, who I've been working with ever since, volunteered with me and we got more and more interested and realized there was a real need in Cleveland to develop some training for this field. We worked through the Garden Center of Greater Cleveland (now known as the Cleveland Botanical Garden) to get some workshops going. We stayed as volunteers until 1981; then Libby and I joined the staff sharing a full-time job between us. We went to them and said that this has gotten too big for us to handle as volunteers. We're spending 20 hours a week apiece on this. If you want to expand this any more and really get into horticultural therapy in a big way, you need a paid position. We helped them design the job and set the salary.

"Over the years we've had quite a varied program through the Garden Center. We contract with different agencies for outreach programs. Typical programs have been at children's hospitals or nursing homes. We'd go every other week and design a year-long curriculum that includes indoor and outdoor gardening. We have activities that involve propagation from seeds and cuttings, or repotting activities. We work with plants as well as dried materials for crafts, pressed flowers and flower arranging and that sort of thing.

"A good 60 percent of our time is spent out in the community. We recently developed a three-year program of intergenerational gardening in a neighborhood center in the inner city. The program brings seniors and elementary school children together.

"We also do a lot of public speaking to garden clubs and civic organizations to help educate people about horticultural therapy and its benefits."

Nancy has also been involved with training future horticultural therapists through the Cleveland Botanical Garden, which offers a six-month internship program. Their address is listed at the end of this chapter.

The Rewards of the Profession

"It certainly isn't money," Nancy Stevenson says. "We're not very well paid. I think the reward for me is being able to combine horticulture and gardening, which have always been very strong interests of mine, with working directly with people— helping people learn about the therapeutic benefits of gardening and how working with plants can help them, no matter what their disability or limitation is.

"I think the relationship between therapist and client is very important. You set up a nonthreatening situation where positive change can occur for someone. You have to build trust."

Friends of Horticultural Therapy

In addition to Nancy Stevenson's active role in the AHTA—she was president from 1989 to 1992 and only recently retired from the board—she is also chairperson of the Friends of Horticultural Therapy, which is an adjunct to the professional organization. "We're involved with public information and fundraising," Nancy explains, "and one of our main purposes is to spread the good word about gardening as therapy—for everyone."

In addition to helping support the goals of the professional association, members of the Friends of Horticultural Therapy receive discounts on garden supplies and seeds, magazines, special rates on conferences, tours, and seminars, and a quarterly newsletter.

You can contact them at the AHTA address listed at the end of this chapter.

The Training You'll Need

Because horticultural therapy is such a young discipline, finding training is not an easy process. Currently, Kansas State University's Department of Horticulture, Forestry, and Recreation Resources is the only bachelor's and master's degree program offered in horticultural therapy in the United States. Three universities, Herbert H. Lehman College, Texas A & M University, and University of Rhode Island (program addresses can be found at the end of this chapter) offer bachelor's degrees in horticulture with options in horticultural therapy. Edmonds Community College awards a two-year AA degree in horticultural therapy and various other institutes such as Massachusetts Bay Community College and Temple University (a list can be found at the end of this chapter) offer horticultural therapy electives.

There are several routes an aspiring horticultural therapist can take to become qualified. Dr. Richard Mattson, a professor at Kansas State University's program, recommends a four-year course of study that covers several disciplines.

"Originally, our program was narrowly defined in that we were training students to work primarily in psychiatric hospitals with mentally ill patients. We have a much broader definition today of horticultural therapy. It's more universal. We feel that the human benefits of gardening that help with issues such as self-esteem and stress-reduction, improve the quality of life. Horticultural therapy is any kind of interaction of people and plants for mutual benefit. So, we work in community gardens or community farmer's markets. Students work in botanical gardens or arboreta, in the public school systems, or within zoo horticulture. They work in vocational training centers or do international placements with the Peace Corps, or in horticultural industry.

"Our concept at Kansas State is that the individual must be trained in a multidisciplinary approach," Dr. Mattson explains. "That means you have to cross over some of the traditional barriers that exist between discipline areas. For example, horticulture is one of the disciplines. Horticulture involves the art and science of growing and culturing plant material in intensive or adapted environments. But then, to work effectively with people, the student must be well-trained in areas of psychology, sociology, and education. We think all of those are important. There are also supporting areas such as human ecology, which used to be called home economics. But it's a very important field because

it deals with the growth and development of family and relationships. Architecture is also important for creating accessible
landscapes. Students can also pursue a number of other areas
such as speech pathology, communications, computer science,
robotics, human anatomy, and muscle movement."

Also through the auspices of Kansas State's program, students
spend a six-month internship gaining practical on-the-job training. Students are supervised by registered horticultural therapists
in established programs and are placed coast to coast, from
Friends Hospital in Philadelphia to the Chicago Botanical
Gardens, or any other number of different settings.

But although desirable, a four-year degree is not necessary to
find work as a horticultural therapist. "There are different levels
of entry into the field," says Dr. Mattson. "In this country there
are a lot of volunteers who belong to garden clubs and master
gardener groups taught by the Cooperative Extension Service.
There are some programs that train at the Associate Arts level,
for people who don't have the extra time to devote to their
training. But I do think that the bachelor's or master's is
important. At some time in the future the entry for many areas
of employment in horticultural therapy will be at the graduate
level. Horticultural therapy is not just making flower arrangements or planting gardens. We feel that a multidiscipline training
will help individuals apply what's best known in all the related
fields. A good example is the importance of business and
marketing skills. Many horticultural therapy programs today are
cost-effective, that is they are self-sufficient. But in order to
utilize the valuable products being produced—whether sacks of
potatoes from a vegetable garden or flowers or a landscaping
service being provided—an individual needs skills in how to
market the product."

The Registration Process

Although not every employer of horticultural therapists requires
registration, being a registered therapist greatly increases your
chances of landing a good job. Registration provides the individual with recognition as an accomplished therapist and helps
to keep the profession's standards high.

There are three levels of registration: The HTT designation is for the technician who has generally gone through a two-year program; the HTR designation is for someone with a bachelor's degree; and the HTM is for the person with multiple years of experience and a graduate degree.

However, becoming a registered horticultural therapist does not require a degree in horticultural therapy. A degree in a related field or a combination of work experience and education can all lead to professional registration.

Decisions about registration are peer-reviewed by a committee from the American Horticultural Therapy Association. They follow a point system, awarding points for the number of years of experience, for publications, for attending seminars, for the number of degrees earned, and other related activities.

Do You Have What It Takes?

In addition to training and experience, horticultural therapists need to have a certain personality make-up.

Nancy Stevenson describes the ideal therapist personality: "It's usually someone who's fairly outgoing and comfortable with people and able to express him- or herself well. You should have a natural bent for teaching and be able to communicate with people to instruct them on basic gardening techniques. It's kind of an elusive quality, but you should have whatever that something is that makes people feel comfortable with you, to be able to talk freely with you. It's similar to the qualities most kinds of therapists should possess.

"I think you also have to be able to stay fairly detached and not get too emotionally involved with the people you're trying to help, otherwise it can be hard on you."

Salaries for Horticultural Therapists

The American Horticultural Therapy Association conducts an annual survey to determine salary levels for nonregistered therapists, HTTs, HTRs, and HTMs. The results of a 1993 poll show that the average salary of therapists with one year or less employment experience is $24,920 per year. Averages go up with the number of years working experience. Therapists can expect to make an average of $26,756 with one to five years of experience, $27,263 with five to ten years of experience, and $33,070 with ten or more years.

Salaries increase by $1,500 to approximately $2,500 or so per year for those who have obtained professional registration.

Further Reading

Directory of Herbal Training Programs, American Herbalist Guild, P.O. Box 1683, Soquel, CA 95073.

"Recommended Reading List," American Herbalist Guild, P.O. Box 1683, Soquel, CA 95073.

For Further Information

Herbalism

American Herbalist Guild
Box 1683
Soquel, CA 95073

Flower Essence Society
P.O. Box 459
Nevada City, CA 95959

Herb Research Foundation
1007 Pearl St., #200
Boulder, CO 80302

National Wildflower Research Center
2600 FM 973 North
Austin, TX 78725-4201

Horticultural Therapy

Contacts
American Horticultural Therapy Association
362A Christopher Ave.
Gaithersburg, MD 20879

Friends of Horticultural Therapy
362A Christopher Ave.
Gaithersburg, MD 20879

Selected Horticultural Therapy Training Programs
Cleveland Botanical Garden
11030 East Blvd.
Cleveland, OH 44106
(Six-month internship program)
Attention: Libby Reavis

Edmonds Community College
20000 68th Ave. West
Lynnwood, WA 98036
(Two-year program in horticultural therapy)

Dr. Richard Mattson, HTM
Kansas State University
Department of Horticulture, Forestry, and Recreation Resources
Throckmorton Hall
Manhattan, KS 66506
(BS and MS program in Horticultural Therapy)

Kansas State University
Office of Distance Learning
Division of Continuing Education
226 College Court Building
Manhattan, KS 66506-6007
(Short-term correspondence course)

Herbert H. Lehamn College
The City University of New York (in cooperation with the New
York Botanical Garden)
250 Bedford Park Blvd., West
Bronx, NY 10468
(BS in horticulture with options in horticultural therapy)

Massachusetts Bay Community College
Wellesley, MA 02181
Attn: Deborah Krause, HTR
(Horticultural therapy electives)

The New York Botanical Garden
200th St. and Southern Blvd.
Bronx, NY 10458-5126
Attn: Rosemary Kern or Joel Flagler
(Certificate Program—179 hours/0.5 points toward AHTA Pro-
fessional Registration)

Rockland Community College
Suffern, NY 10901
Attn: Dr. Bill Baker
(Horticultural therapy electives)

Temple University
Department of Landscape Architecture and Horticulture
Ambler, PA 19002
Attn: John F. Collins
(Horticultural therapy electives)

Tennessee Technological University
School of Agriculture
Box 5034
Cookerville, TN 38505
Attn: Dr. Douglas Airhart, HTM
(Horticultural therapy electives)

Texas A & M University
Department of Horticulture
College Station, TX 77843-2133
(BS in horticulture with options in horticultural therapy)

Tulsa Junior College
Northeast Campus
Department of Science and Engineering
3727 East Apache
Tulsa, OK 74115
Attn: John Kahre, Assistant Director
(Horticultural therapy electives)

University of Massachusetts
Department of Plant & Soil Science
Durfee Conservatory, French Hall
Amherst, MA 01002
Attn: John Tristan, MS, HTR
(Horticultural therapy electives)

University of Rhode Island
Department of Plant Science
Kingston, RI 02881
(BS in horticulture with options in horticultural therapy)

Virginia Polytechnic Institute and State University
Department of Horticulture
Blacksburg, VA 24061
Attn: Dr. P.D. Relf, HTM
(Horticultural therapy electives)

CHAPTER SEVEN

Garden Writers and Photographers

C ombining your knowledge and love of plants with a talent for writing and/or photography can bring in extra income or result in a full-time career. With a thorough grasp of your subject, an understanding of the needs of book publishers and magazine and newspaper editors, and a lot of drive and persistence, dedicated plant lovers can teach others what they know through written words and photographic images.

Writing About Plants

Writing "How-To" Books

Investigate any bookstore or your local library and you'll find hundreds of volumes covering every aspect of the world of plants, from growing specific flowers such as roses or tulips to how to design a rooftop garden or establish a career for yourself in the field.

These "how-to" books can be very successful and publishers are always on the lookout for new projects that take a fresh approach. Here are just a few well-covered topics:

Annuals

Bonsai creations

Container gardens (from pottery to toilet bowls)

Garden crafts

Garden feeding

Garden pests

Herb gardens

House plants

Lilies

Orchids

Perennials

Roses

Vegetables

Vines

Wildflowers

Deciding on a Topic

When deciding about what to write, it's a good idea to find a topic that has not been overdone. An overlooked subject or a new slant or twist on an old subject can work; the trick is to find a hole in the marketplace, a gap that only your book can fill.

If you've come across a gap and thought of the perfect idea for a book to fill it, don't worry if you think your experience or knowledge is too limited. Very few writers can put together a book without doing research or interviewing experts in the field. Professional associations can direct you to members who would be willing to help.

Getting Started

After you've developed your idea and have checked to make sure it brings something new to the market, you need to prepare a book proposal. Your proposal will state your topic, why your book has something different to offer, who will buy your book, and what format your book will take. You'll need a table of contents, a sample chapter or two, and an outline of the remaining chapters. An excellent resource to guide you is Michael Larsen's book *How to Write a Book Proposal* (Writer's Digest Books). In addition to explaining the proper format and content for a book proposal, it also helps you decide if your idea is a viable one.

What to Do with Your Book Proposal

While you were studying the variety of titles already out there, you were taking note of the particular publishing houses that had put them in print. Your book proposal has to be sent to publishers who handle your topic. Inappropriate submissions waste everyone's time and your postage. You can write to the various publishers for their catalogs; this will give you an idea of their full range and will show you where your title might fit their list. You can also study the *Writers Market* (Writers Digest Books), an annual guide that lists publishers and their needs and requirements.

Some writers prefer to concentrate on their writing (and their gardening), and they work with agents who handle the selling side. Finding an agent can take almost as much time as finding a publisher, but in the end, it is well worth the effort. A good agent knows what projects will fit with which publishers—and which will not. You can find an agent through *The Literary Marketplace*, (R. R. Bowker), available at your library, or through Writer's Digest's *Guide to Literary Agents & Art/Photo Reps*. You can also write to the AAR (Association of Authors' Representatives), 10 Astor Place, 3rd Floor, New York, NY 10003, for a list of its member agents. AAR members agree to adhere to a specific code of ethics; the AAR's list, however, does not specify areas of interest.

What Happens Next?

Once your proposal has been submitted, the waiting begins. If your project grabs the right editor's interest, if you've presented your subject well and have made a convincing argument for the viability of your project—and you've been lucky—you might be asked to submit the completed manuscript for consideration. The best-case scenario would be an acceptance based upon your proposal. Successful writers know that there are two keys to joining the ranks of published authors:

1. An interesting and well-executed manuscript/proposal and

2. persistence.

If your idea is a good one, the quality of your work is exceptional, and you don't give up easily, approaching a publisher can eventually pay off.

David Hirsch, Gardener, Chef, and Author

David Hirsch has been with Moosewood Restaurant, a collectively-run vegetarian eating establishment in Ithaca, New York, for almost 20 years. Moosewood opened its doors in 1973 and was at first known only locally. Now, two decades and several highly-acclaimed cookbooks later, Moosewood's reputation for serving fine food in a friendly atmosphere has spread nationally.

David collaborated with other collective members to write *New Recipes from Moosewood Restaurant, Sundays at Moosewood Restaurant,* and *Moosewood Restaurant Cooks at Home.* (David Hirsch and how Moosewood Restaurant began are profiled in *Careers for Health Nuts*—see "Further Reading" at the end of this chapter.)

David is also the author of *The Moosewood Restaurant Kitchen Garden,* a practical guide to creative gardening for the adventurous cook. While sharing his personal experiences with the reader, David gives instructions for growing and harvesting, creating garden design plans, and using more than 30 vegetables and 35 herbs including edible flowers and gourmet vegetables. Also included is a chapter of recipes that puts your garden's yield to good use.

The book has been well-received with more than 50,000 copies in print.

David talks about his book and how he got started: "Even when I was a kid growing up in Bayside, Queens we had this little postage-stamp in front of the house and I used to plant seeds and water them. I wasn't an adventurous gardener then, but I enjoyed it and I had that sense of continuity of taking care of something.

"For me there was always a very strong connection between the process of growing and cooking and these are two areas that strongly interest me. I love to garden and I love to cook. It seemed as if it would be a very enjoyable project, to take two things I cared about and knew a fair amount about and write about them.

"We already had literary agents because of the other Moosewood books and they suggested I write a proposal. I put it together and they submitted it to Simon & Schuster.

"It's always nice to make money at something you love, but as with any job, there are always some stresses or concerns. For me, there was certainly the concern of writing a whole book by myself. But I did get a lot of support. Other Moosewood people helped out and tested my recipes. Writing requires a real commitment of time and space to get it done. You have deadlines hanging over your head all the way through. The publishers want half the manuscript by a certain date, the remaining half by another date. Then you send it in and they send it back to you with suggestions for changes and another deadline they want to receive everything by. So you have to set up that discipline in your life.

"A lot of people who aren't full-time writers are doing something else with their time. You have to work around that to fit everything in."

Some Advice from David

"Pick an area that interests you, an area you want to learn more about, because with most writing projects you have to do some research. You need to know something about the subject, you need to have something to say.

"In terms of marketing, what you have to say should have some angle that's different from what's already out there. There must be hundreds of books on house plants, for example, but recently I purchased two books on the subject that approached things for a different perspective. One was a book on fragrant house plants; the other talks about landscaping the interior of your house. What a writer has to do is take a unique perspective and work with that."

SOME TOPIC SUGGESTIONS

Colonial gardening

Garden structures (arbors, fences, gazebos, trellises, etc.)

Herbal medicines

Indoor citrus plants

Natural plant communities

New design plans for the garden

Regional gardening

Writing Articles for Magazines and Newspapers

For those of you who feel tackling a book-length project seems too overwhelming, at least at first, you can always start with magazine and newspaper articles. There are hundreds of magazines that, if not entirely devoted to plants, include some kind of gardening or plant section for their readership. Take a look at any good-size newsstand, make note of gardening magazines; then flip through other general interest publications to see which ones also include articles on plants or gardening. The *Writer's Market*, in addition to listing book publishers and their requirements, also contains a hefty selection of both trade and consumer publications.

Most major newspapers and many local ones have gardening sections or columns. Although these are often written by full-time staffers, some newspapers are open to freelance submissions. You can find a listing of newspapers in your library. Abalone Press has compiled a computerized directory on disk of the nation's biggest dailies, complete with the names of nearly 2,000 key editors. It is formatted to work with whatever word processing or database program you use and can save you hours of unnecessary typing while sending out multiple submissions. For more information you can contact Abalone Press at 14 Hickory Ave., Takoma Park, MD 20912.

How to Get Started Freelancing

You don't have to work full-time for a publication to write plant-related articles; most magazines use a good number of freelance submissions each month. Most freelancers work as independent contractors, setting up a home office, sending out article ideas or completed manuscripts, negotiating payment, and setting their own hours. Of course, there are deadlines to meet and a publishable standard of work to deliver.

Editors want to see well-written, informative articles that will be of interest to their readers. A good article should have a strong lead and a body filled with examples, anecdotes, and quotes from experts.

How Much You'll Be Paid

Payment for one article varies from publication to publication, but could range from $50 or so for small magazines, to $200 or $300, up to $1,000 or more for national magazines. Some magazines pay you as soon as they've accepted your manuscript; others wait until your article has been published.

The trick to making enough money is to allow one article to bring in more than one fee. As long as the publications do not have a competing circulation, and you haven't sold all rights to the article, you can place your work more than once. For example, an article on house plants and air conditioning could find homes in several regional magazines in the South, as well as with local newspapers.

Reslanting an article to capture a broader audience can also help increase your salary. An article on teaching children how to care for plants can be rewritten to address a novice adult audience. Reslanting increases the number of publications you can approach; resales increase your paycheck.

Some Sample Markets

In addition to a wide variety of national magazines that cover everything from azaleas to zinnias, most states have regional magazines with garden features. The following is a small sampling of publications that accept articles on plants from freelance writers:

American Horticulturist (for advanced gardeners)

Better Homes and Gardens

Carolina Gardener

Colorado Homes and Lifestyles

Country Journal

Fine Gardening

Florida Home and Garden

Flower and Garden Magazine

Garden Design

The Growing Edge

Harrowsmith Country Life

The Herb Companion

Horticulture

House and Garden

HousePlant Magazine

National Gardening

Natural Food and Farming

New Jersey Monthly

Organic Gardening

Texas Gardener

Your Home

Approaching Editors

There are different ways to approach a publication; the method you choose should follow the preferences the editors have expressed in the various market books or in their own guidelines for writers. To get a copy of a magazine's guidelines, send your request with an SASE (self-addressed stamped envelope).

It is also a good idea to have read the magazine for which you would like to write so you are familiar with its format and style.

If you can't find the magazine at a newsstand, you can write the publishers for a sample copy.

The first rule when approaching a magazine is to make sure your letter is addressed to a specific editor by name. You can find this information in the magazine's masthead, or listed in the *Writer's Market*.

Some editors don't want to see an entire article right away; they would rather you send them a query letter. A query letter is a miniproposal, stating the topic about which you would like to write, how you would approach it, and what qualifies you to write it. The query letter gives the editor an idea of your writing style and helps him or her decide quickly if the subject matter is right for the publication. You might be proposing an article they've already covered or have plans to cover with a different writer. Query letters save everyone time.

If an editor likes your query, you'll probably receive a letter asking to see the completed manuscript. New freelancers just breaking in often have to write the article "on spec" with no guarantee of publication. Once you have some publishing credits under your belt, a query letter can lead to a paid assignment.

Other editors will bypass the query stage and ask to see the entire manuscript first.

Once your piece has been accepted, be prepared to wait several months before it sees print, although newspapers usually have a faster turn around time than magazines.

Landing a Regular Column

Once a freelancer has established herself, she can often land regular assignments with the same editors. This can even turn into a permanent column in a magazine or newspaper. And a writer can syndicate herself, selling the same column to newspapers across the country.

Garden columnists write about various topics or answer readers' questions.

A Garden Writer

When Robert (Bob) Haehle opens up his daily mail he's never quite sure what he'll receive. "This is the grimmer side of my job," Bob explains. "People send me dead leaves or bits of fruit and seeds. Sometimes I get squashed bugs. They have only three legs remaining and they were sent wrapped in plastic, so they're moldy and a terrible mess by the time I get them. You never know what's coming in the next load."

Bob is not the brunt of a harassment campaign; he writes a weekly question-and-answer format garden column for the *Fort Lauderdale Sun-Sentinel*, a newspaper with a circulation of more than 300,000. "I've developed a following. Readers cut out the columns and save them in scrap books. It's nice to know you're helping people."

Bob answers all questions that are sent to him. "Sometimes I have to play detective, to figure out what plants they're referring to; people use all sorts of different regional names. And with certain problems, I can refer to my own garden. I have a collection of one of this or one of that—from a landscape point of view it might not always flow together that well, but for a study tool and a research tool, to know what's going on at any given time of the year, it's great to have all these things in the yard."

Questions range from how to protect backyard citrus trees from disease to how to encourage blossoms from a bird of paradise. (For best results for the latter situation, Bob recommends allowing the family dog to help with the watering.)

"South Florida is a very special area," Bob says, "horticulturally different from the rest of the United States, with the exception of Hawaii. There really aren't a lot of gardening books dealing with all the conditions here. An incredible number of people move down here every year, but they're coming from different parts of the country and don't know what they're getting into. They may have gardened up north, but here you could almost literally say that conditions are 180 degrees different from the way they are in other locales. Up north it's acid soil; down here it's alkaline soil. Up north you plant your vegetables and annuals around May or so, and they're finished around October; here we plant them in October and usually get two crops, and then by April or May they're ready to pack it in. There are so many differences."

In addition to his column, Bob also regularly writes articles for the paper covering topics from roses and seashore gardening to storm damage control and the proper pruning of trees.

He also freelances for a variety of regional magazines such as *Florida Nurseryman* and *South Florida Home and Garden* in addition to working with Time-Life garden encyclopedias.

Condominium complexes also hire Bob as a horticultural consultant for advice on landscaping and other concerns. "I advise them if they have any insect or disease problems. I give landscape recommendations, fertilization recommendations—all in a written report format."

And every week, South Florida residents can find Bob at a local nursery running a plant clinic.

The reason for all the activity, besides his love of what he's doing, is that it's difficult to make a living at freelance garden writing alone.

"I make about $100 a week for the column, maybe $150 for articles," Bob says. "I enjoy writing, but only more or less when I feel like doing it. Someone more ambitious than I could probably make a full-time career out of it. They could work fulltime on the staff of a paper, for example, but that's too structured for me.

"It's been my observation that the real horticulturists, the people who really love plants, normally are not great business people. They tend to be much more giving and sharing then your average hard-hearted attorney out for blood; we're at the other end of the spectrum. And I would say that most horticulturalists who really like what they do are not necessarily motivated by material possessions or financial gain. We can be viewed as somewhat eccentric when it comes to gardens. But in horticulture, whatever aspect you go into, if you also have a business orientation you can probably do okay."

Bob is overly modest about his background, which is more than impressive. He has a bachelor's degree from the University of Massachusetts in environmental design/landscape architecture and a master's degree from the University of Delaware in horticulture and botanic garden management.

He has worked as an educational horticulturist at Brookside Gardens outside of Washington D.C., giving lectures and putting out a newsletter, and later as director of the facility. He took classes in horticultural writing during his master's program and also co-hosted a radio phone-in show called "Plant Talk."

"You don't necessarily have to have a horticultural background to be a garden writer, but it does help. You should have a good background in English, and also have some interviewing skills for doing articles. It's also important to build up a good personal library of key reference books."

You can find Bob Haehle's column every Friday in the *Fort Lauderdale Sun-Sentinel*.

Photographing Plants

Plant lovers with photographic skills can create a career for themselves as freelancers or by teaming up with garden writers to illustrate magazine and newspaper articles or "how-to" books.

Photographers also put their talents to good use photographing material for catalogs that florists use to advertise their floral arrangements.

Photographers generally set their own hours and can travel to different locations, chronicling flower shows or regional foliage. In addition to books and articles, they also produce photographs for calendars, art posters, and postcards.

A Floral Photographer

In addition to his role as director of the American Floral Art School (you will find information on the school in Chapter Two under the heading of "Training for Floral Designers"), James (Jim) Moretz is also a professional floral photographer and floral designer who contributes photographs and articles on floral design to trade magazines around the world. His work has appeared in the United States, Canada, Taiwan, Japan, Switzerland, and Holland. He is also the author of *Posey Bouquet Holders, An Alluring Victorian Fashion; Creative and Commercial Floral Design*; and *Creative Floral Design* (in Chinese.)

Here Jim gives some valuable tips for budding photographers:

Professional-looking floral photographs can be used to record design ideas, for a design portfolio, for publicity and advertising, for personal recognition, to sell from, to study design elements, and for Phase I AIFD requirements (explained in Chapter Two under the heading of "Training for Floral Designers").

Taking a great floral photograph requires expertise both in art and technique, just as they are needed in making a great floral design.

Good pictures just don't happen. So many variables have to be considered and controlled—kind and speed of film, shutter speed, amount and quality of light, and the size of lens opening (f-stop).

For beginners, simplicity in cameras and accessories is best. Four basic items are necessary to take good floral pictures:

1. A 35mm single-lens reflex camera (SLR) with built-in light meter, manual focus, a 50mm lens with f-stops going to f-22 or f-32, and a manual shutter with speeds up to 1/8 or 1/16 seconds.

2. Color film in the 50 to 200 ISO film speed is best for most applications. Generally, the slower the film (low ISO number) the finer the detail and less grain showing in the enlarged print. Negative print film is best unless specific use calls for color slides for color magazine publication.

3. and 4. A sturdy tripod and cable release are absolutely necessary. The average person cannot hold a camera steady below 1/30th of a second. With low light levels, slow shutter speeds are necessary to maintain a high f-stop. A cable release prevents moving or jarring the camera during exposure.

Here are some other points to consider for good photography:

Light The brighter and more diffused the light source, the better the photograph and the less distracting the shadows. Avoid flash pictures. Diffuse the light indoors by using umbrellas. Two or more lights are better than one.

Exposure Floral designs have depth. To keep all the flowers in focus (from the front to the back of the design), it is necessary to use the highest f-stop (lens opening of f-16 to f-22 or more).

The higher the f-stop the more "depth of field," or better focus, the lens produces on the film.

Backgrounds Backgrounds should be simple, uncluttered, and nondistracting. Plain walls, seamless photographic paper, non-reflective fabric, foam boards, or painted backgrounds work well.

Composition Place the camera and tripod at eye level. A camera placed too low will overemphasize the container and distort the design. Most flower designs look best photographed vertically unless the arrangement is wider than tall. Fill the frame. Leave "breathing room" around the four edges of the subject. Isolate the subject. Designs touching or crowded together on a table make a poor picture.

Training for Photographers

Some photographers are self-taught while others attend college or art school. Still others find a professional photographer with whom they can apprentice.

Floral photographers need to become familiar with all the technical as well as artistic aspects of photography. A part of any training program would include studying what other photographers produce.

Photographers with some market savvy also recognize the importance of acquiring good writing skills. This way they are able to write their own articles to go with their pictures, thus increasing their income.

Salaries

Payment varies from assignment to assignment and from publication to publication. Sometimes a photographer will be paid a set amount for each photograph that eventually sees print. That amount will also vary depending on the size of the photograph, whether it, for example, fills a quarter, half, or full page. Photographs that make the cover of a magazine earn more.

Sometimes a photographer will work on an hourly or day rate. An editor might agree to pay for two full days of work at a set fee.

If the assignment takes longer, the photographer will not earn any more money for that particular job. At the same time, if she spends less time than she originally planned, she is not expected to refund any of the fee.

In addition to their fee, photographers usually are paid for any additional expenses such as travel and lodging or renting extra equipment or props.

Further Reading

Careers for Health Nuts, by Blythe Camenson, NTC Publishing.

The Floral Designers' Guide to Photography, by William T. & Frances L. Bode, House of Bode, 2800 Huntington Rd., Sacramento, CA 95864, 1988.

Guide to Literary Agents and Art/Photo Reps, an annual from Writer's Digest Books.

How to Photograph Flowers, Plants & Landscapes, by Derek Fell, H.P. Books, P.O. Box 5367, Tucson, AZ 85703, 1980.

How to Write a Book Proposal, by Michael Larsen, Writer's Digest Books, 1985.

How to Write Irresistible Query Letters, by Lisa Collier Cool, Writer's Digest Books, 1987.

Moosewood Restaurant Cooks at Home, by the Moosewood Collective, Simon & Schuster, 1994.

The Moosewood Restaurant Kitchen Garden, by David Hirsch, Simon & Schuster, 1992.

Photographer's Market, Writer's Digest Books. A comprehensive listing of more than 2,500 U.S. and international buyers of freelance photographs. Each listing gives the name and address of the buyer, how to submit your photos, what kind of photos they buy, pay rates, and tips about how to break in.

New Recipes From Moosewood Restaurant, by the Moosewood Collective, Ten Speed Press, 1987.

Sundays At Moosewood Restaurant, by the Moosewood Collective, Simon & Schuster, 1990.

Writer's Market, an annual from Writer's Digest Books.

For Further Information

Garden Writers Association of America
c/o Robert La Gasse
10210 Leatherleaf Court
Manassas, VA 22111

American Society of Media Photographers
14 Washington Rd., Ste. 502
Princeton Junction, NJ 08550

CHAPTER EIGHT

Careers with Edible Plants

A t the heart of our economic structure are American farmers, who operate one of the world's largest and most productive agricultural industries. They produce enough food to meet the needs of our country and to export huge quantities to countries around the world.

Farm can be huge conglomerates, or small privately or cooperatively owned enterprises. Farmers can also be tenant farmers, renting the land they use.

Working with Edible Plants

Duties

Within the field of agriculture there are a number of different occupations. On the production side there are the growers, owners, managers, and field hands. Once the food has been harvested experienced handlers store it, then pack and ship it. Distributors handle sales and marketing, and retailers such as restaurants and supermarkets sell to the public.

The specific tasks for growers are determined by the type of farm. On traditional crop farms, operators are responsible for planning, tilling, planting, fertilizing, cultivating, spraying, and harvesting. Organic farmers, who do not use chemicals in their operations, must also seek out alternative ways to fight pests and disease and increase production.

On large farms owners or managers spend time meeting with supervisors and traveling between the field and their offices.

Training for Farmers

Modern farming requires complex scientific, business, and financial decisions. Today's farmer must acquire a strong educational background. It is no longer enough to grow up on a farm or participate as a youth in 4-H activities, though these are important contributors to an overall education.

For those who have no previous farming experience, a bachelor's degree in agriculture is essential. To qualify as a manager, several years' experience in different phases of farm operation would also be necessary.

Students should choose a college appropriate to their specific interests and location. All states have land-grant colleges with agriculture departments. For crop growers, courses would cover agricultural economics, crop and fruit science, and soil science.

Farm operators and managers need to keep informed of continuing advances in farming methods. They should be willing to try new techniques and adapt to constantly changing technologies to produce their crops.

They should also be familiar with the different farm machinery and its safe use as well as with chemicals and their applications.

Accounting and bookkeeping are also important skills. And these days, more and more farms are depending upon computers to keep track of accounts and crop production and distribution.

Farm managers need to have business skills, good communication skills, and marketing and sales experience.

Finger Lakes Organic Growers Cooperative

The Finger Lakes Organic Growers is a cooperative enterprise with approximately thirty active members. Most of the farms, which are spread across New York State, are 15 acres or smaller. Each grower has purchased shares in the cooperative and the cooperative in exchange markets their produce for them.

Their aim is to grow all their crops organically without the use of any chemical pesticides or fertilizers. They are committed to sustainable agriculture, meaning they farm in such a way that the environment benefits from it—the soil gets richer and the general ecology is preserved.

Carol Stull, Grower

Carol Stull is one of the founding members of the Finger Lakes Organic Growers Cooperative, which began operation in 1986. "It actually started under the black locust tree in my backyard," Carol explains. "There had been a group of growers, about six of us, that had been meeting and talking about how running around and trying to sell everything ourselves was a hassle. Several of our regular customers would buy one thing from someone, but if they ran out, they'd go to someone else. So our thinking was that if we could go together it would be more expeditious.

"We had been talking about it for a year and then one of the growers said, 'Let's do it and here's my $5 to start.' We used that to mail out the minutes. Then we applied for a grant from New York State Agriculture and Markets. At the time they had money they'd gotten from the federal government for grants.

"We got $15,000 and we used it as start up money for the cooperative. We set up a computer program and we rented a truck for deliveries. The market manager worked out of her living room then. That first year we didn't even have a warehouse—we used a farm that belonged to one of our growers and we brought things there or to a couple of pickup points. We were pretty low-budget, but we were able to pay an artist to develop our logo and to get office supplies. And also, when you sell things, there's a delay between the time you sell and the time you get the money so we used some of the grant to cover employees' salaries.

"Each member has his own farm. Right at the beginning one of the things we decided is that we couldn't compete with each other in the marketplace. We got advice from a Vista volunteer who worked with another cooperative, and learned that we should, for example, set up a personnel committee so every grower wasn't telling the manager something different to do. We each gave up all our wholesale markets to the co-op. It used to cost us at least a quarter of our time to do the selling, and that really wasn't enough to do it right. So we've changed that now and the manager takes care of all of that."

CAROL'S INDIVIDUAL FARM   Carol and her husband bought their land in Ithaca, New York in 1985. "Our business was only a year old when we started the cooperative. Before that we used to market our produce direct at farmer's markets. We were small, just learning to go from packets to pounds. You buy a packet of seeds for a small home garden, but when you're growing commercially you buy seeds by the pound. We have 65 acres and farm about 10 acres of it. We grow all of the standard vegetables, except corn. We have a problem with deer.

"One of the reasons I like doing this is that I can grow any weird thing I want. That was one of our entries into the wholesale restaurant market. I can grow edible flowers or unusual cherry tomatoes that other people don't grow. We also grow a lot of herbs; seven or eight different basils, for example.

"The number of employees I have fluctuates. In the summer I hire students. We have about eight who help with the planting and picking. It's a lot easier if you have several thousand tomato plants and six or eight people to chat with as you're picking. Then it can be fun work. By yourself it's a lot harder.

"I do all the planning. We grow a lot of different crops, so we have to know where they're going to go. We do a three-year rotation, which means we don't plant crops from the same family in the same place in the field for three years.

"There's a lot of planning and a lot of adjusting to your planning if things don't work out—whether it's the weather that doesn't cooperate or the equipment breaks down or someone doesn't show up or things grow faster or slower than you thought they would. You spend a lot of time figuring out what you're doing. We have 187 different food products, and a wide line of perennials and herb plants and that's a lot going on.

"We have three greenhouses and in the winter I grow a lot of salad greens for the hotel school at Cornell."

Carol also sells at the local farmer's market on Saturdays and has a roadside stand on her property. "When you have more cherry tomatoes than you absolutely know what to do with you look at every market available."

CAROL'S BACKGROUND   Carol was trained as a clinical chemist with a biology background and she worked eighteen years as a hospital chemist. Her bachelor's degree is from the University of Illinois and her master's is from Baylor in Texas.

Although she grew up in suburban Evanston, Illinois, there's been a farm in her family since her great grandfather's time.

Carol loves farming. "We have a very inspiring view. Our farm sits on top of a hill overlooking twenty miles of Cayuga Lake. If you're feeling a little down in the morning the view will perk you up.

"But what I like most is the fascination of seeing a little seedling transfer into something big, watching the flowers open up. Then seeing the fruits of your labor when you go out and start harvesting. The little plants you transplanted are now ready to be eaten or sold or whatever you're going to do with them. It's a thrill."

Sally Miller, Manager of Finger Lakes Organic Growers Cooperative

The Finger Lakes Organic Growers employ a full-time marketing manager, an assistant manager, and a warehouse manager who is responsible for quality control and putting the orders together to go out on the trucks. The work is seasonable and the managers are on shorter schedules in the winter.

Sally Miller is the cooperative's marketing manager. "My main function is the marketing and advertising," Sally explains. "We try to expand the business. The board of directors meets once a month to do long-term strategic planning with our recommendations. If they decide they want to expand, say 20 percent with new customers, then it's the manager's job to decide how to do that."

Thousands of bushels go through their warehouse every year and this year they're expecting to gross about $400,000 in sales.

"We supply to restaurants, supermarkets, retail food co-ops, and natural food stores, and to other wholesalers when we have a surplus of something. For example, zucchini tends to grow all at once and it's doing that right now. We have so much that I can lower the price and make it appealing to other wholesalers who might not have enough of a supply.

"Very few people do standing orders. The prices change every week and most restaurants change their side orders—that's what we supply—from week to week. And there's a lot of competition. All the customers get different price lists every week and then they decide who they're going to buy from. We fax price lists and follow up with a call. Some of our customers, such as Moosewood Restaurant, are nearby so we can figure out what they need and drop it off on our way home from work. Locally we know all the people we're selling to.

"For customers farther away we have an arrangement for shipping with the people we share warehouse space with. They're Regional Access, a natural food wholesaler and we rent their truck. A lot of time we ship to a lot of the same customers.

"In addition to the marketing, I do a certain amount of educating about new crops, how to store them and display them. We put out a newsletter and do all the bookkeeping, anything that goes into a business.

"One of the things our cooperative is famous for is very good hands-on quality control, so we spend a lot of time in the cooler examining the produce. Then when a customer calls we can tell him that we have great red leaf lettuce, for example. The heads are small but they're holding together very well. We try to give a lot of information. Or we share information about what's moving well or not moving at different food co-ops. There are always trends. Asparagus is something people buy like crazy—they love it. So if you have asparagus you know they'll have no trouble selling it. But then something like chard, which was very popular when I first started working here—it's a gorgeous thing and has long leaves and you can chop it up and use it in stirfries—is becoming less and less popular and there's no real reason why.

"We end up talking about the weather a lot, too. People might mention casually that it's been real hot. And then we say, 'Yes, and that's why we don't have any lettuce. Not only are you suffering, but all of our lettuce has bolted—gone to seed—and it doesn't taste good anymore.

"We take the orders and keep track to make sure we're not running out of things. The warehouse manager comes in and gets the invoices and then goes into the cooler and stacks the boxes together on a truck pallet, ready to go out. Then our trucker loads up and drives off.

"Sometimes things go wrong with the orders and we deal with that. Someone got something they weren't expecting or their bananas were too ripe and they want a discount. And there's always mediation between customers and growers. Your customers don't necessarily know how agriculture works; your growers don't understand marketing. So you help resolve any disputes."

SALLY'S BACKGROUND   Sally spent eight years earning her doctorate in anthropology at Cornell University in Ithaca, New York. She finished in January, 1992, but by May she felt as if she'd had enough. "I realized I didn't want to spend my life teaching. I don't think I was really cut out for it. But the degree gave me a lot of experience that I use now; doing interviews, writing a project yourself, getting funding, writing grants, which is a kind of marketing.

"I had done a lot of volunteer work at Greenstar, the local food co-op. I loved it and realized that that was what I wanted to do. Originally, I was looking for a farming job but there weren't any; then this job came along and I started in May of 1992.

"What I'm doing here seems more real for me. In some ways it was a political decision. I feel I'm doing more now because I'm working with a lot of people who are doing sustainable agriculture, trying to preserve the land and not putting pesticides into the air. Organic farming is a very difficult business; they tend to be small family farms and they go out of business all the time. And if I can sell a lot of their produce and get good prices for them, then maybe that's one farm that doesn't go out of business this year.

"I love marketing, talking to the customers. Some of them I've known for a long time and they trust me to make sure their produce looks good. And I trust them to go on buying from me and not switch to other suppliers. You tend to develop good relationships that way.

"There's some stress to the job. Last week we had 150 cases of lettuce come in and that was about 20 times the amount we had the week before. I was worried about whether or not it would all sell, but it was exciting, too. And it did all sell.

"If it hadn't sold, I would've had to compost it all and tell the growers. If you've had a stressful day it's a good way to get over it, carrying out the slimy lettuce to the compost heap."

Earnings

Income for farmers can vary from year to year. Food prices fluctuate from week to week and are affected by the weather and other factors that influence the demand for certain products. The size and type of farm also affects income. Generally, large farms produce more income than smaller operations. The exception to that are specialty farms producing small amounts of high-value horticultural and fruit products.

According to the U.S. Department of Agriculture, average income after expenses for operators of vegetable and fruit farms was $100,000 in 1993. Individual income can vary widely. Sally Miller, the manager of the Finger Lakes Organic Growers earns $8.25 an hour; her assistant manager started out at $6.50 an hour and will go up to $7 or $7.50 after she's been on board for awhile.

Carol Stull's seasonal workers earn between minimum wage and about $5 an hour. The growers within the cooperative earn different amounts depending upon the size of their property or what kind of year they had. The earnings could range from just $1,000 to about $35,000 or $40,000 in gross sales. Carol's own farm grosses about $25,000 to $30,000 a year. "People don't realize how much it costs people to grow food," Carol says. "I'm still selling things at the same price I was ten years ago because that's what people expect to pay. But ten years ago the minimum wage was lower; now it's gone up and I pay workman's compensation and social security, too.

"It's what I do for a living but my husband also has a full-time job outside the farm. I wouldn't be able to do this at this level if it were just me. As you pay off your equipment and mortgage you have a little more left over for your own salary but it's not easy."

Because the work for some farmers and managers is seasonal, and the income fluctuates so, many growers take second jobs during the off months.

Job Outlook

Employment of farm managers and operators is expected to decline through the year 2005. With an expanding world population there is an increasing demand for food, but because of the efficiency of the American agricultural sector, fewer farms are needed to meet that demand. The overwhelming majority of job openings will come about because of the need to replace farmers who retire or leave the occupation for economic or other reasons.

The trend toward fewer but larger farms is expected to continue to reduce the number of jobs. Small and medium-size farms, many of which do not generate enough income to support their owners, are expected to decrease in number.

However, the increase in the size of farms, generally through mergers, and the higher level of technology being employed in farm work are expected to spur a need for highly trained and experienced farm managers.

For Further Information

For general information about farm occupations, opportunities, and 4-H activities, contact your local Cooperative Extension Service (highlighted in Chapter Five).

The following sources can also provide information about farming and agricultural occupations:

American Farm Bureau Federation
225 Touhy Ave.
Park Ridge, IL 60068

American Farmland Trust
1920 N St., N.W., Ste. 400
Washington, D.C. 20036

American Society of Farm Managers and Rural Appraisers
950 South Cherry St., Ste. 106
Denver, CO 80222

Crop Society of America
677 South Segoe Rd.
Madison, WI 53711

Food and Agricultural Careers for Tomorrow
Purdue University
127 Agricultural Administration Building
West Lafayette, IN 47907

Institute for Alternative Agriculture
9200 Edmonton Rd., Ste. 117
Greenbelt, MD 20770

Institute for Food Technologists
221 N. LaSalle St., Ste. 300
Chicago, IL 60601

National Association of State Departments of Agriculture
1616 H St., N.W.
Washington, D.C. 20006

National Farmers Union
10065 E. Harvard Ave.
Denver, CO 80231

National Future Farmers of America Organization
P.O. Box 15160
National FFA Center
Alexandria, VA 22309

North American Farm Alliance
P.O. Box 2502
Ames, IA 50010

Northeast Organic Farming Association (NOFA)
P.O. Box 21
South Butler, NY 13154

Selected List of Botanical Gardens and Arboreta

Most botanical gardens and arboreta offer opportunities for plant lovers to gain hands-on experience through student internships, summer employment, and volunteer programs. The American Association of Botanical Gardens and Arboreta (AABGA) publishes a directory of more than 500 programs at 125 institutions throughout the country. Information about ordering this directory is listed at the end of Chapter Four. What follows is a selected list of gardens you can contact on your own.

Alaska Botanical Garden
P.O. Box 202202
Anchorage, AK 99520

Andrews University Campus
    Arboretum
Biology Department
Andrews University
Berrien Springs, MI 49104

The Arboretum at Flagstaff
P.O. Box 670
Flagstaff, AZ 86002

Arboretum of the Barnes
    Foundation
P.O. Box 128
Merion Station, PA 19066

Atlanta Botanical Garden
P.O. Box 77246
Atlanta, GA 30357

Auburn University Arboretum
Department of Botany and
    Microbiology
Auburn, AL 36849-5407

Bartlett Arboretum
University of Connecticut
151 Brookdale Rd.
Stamford, CT 06903

Bayou Bend Gardens
1 Westcott
Houston, TX 77007

Berkshire Botanical Garden
P.O. Box 826
Stockbridge, MA 01262

Bernheim Arboretum and Research
    Forest
Highway 245
Clermont, KY 40110

The Berry Botanic Garden
11505 S.W. Summerville Ave.
Portland, OR 97219

Bickelhaupt Arboretum
340 S. 14th St.
Clinton, IA 52732

Blithewold Gardens and Arboretum
101 Ferry Rd.
P.O. Box 716
Bristol, RI 02809-0716

Boerner Botanical Gardens
Milwaukee County Parks Dept.
5879 S. 92nd St.
Hales Corners, WI 53130

Brookgreen Gardens
1931 Brookgreen Gardens Dr.
Murrells Inlet, SC 29576

Brooklyn Botanic Garden
1000 Washington Ave.
Brooklyn, NY 11225-1099

Cape Fear Botanical Garden
P.O. Box 53485
Fayetteville, NC 28305

Chautauqua Arboretum
P.O. Box 231
Crystal Springs, MS 39059

Cheekwood Botanical Gardens
1200 Forrest Park Dr.
Nashville, TN 37205

Cheyenne Botanic Garden
710 South Lion Parks Dr.
Cheyenne, WY 82001

Chicago Botanic Garden
P.O. Box 400
Glencoe, IL 60022-0400

Dyck Arboretum of the Plains
Hession College
Box 3000
Hession, KS 67062

Flamingo Gardens
3750 Flamingo Rd.
Fort Lauderdale, FL 33330

Folsom Children's Zoo & Botanical
Gardens
1222 South 27th St.
Lincoln, NE 68502

Fullerton Arboretum
California State University
Fullerton, CA 92634

Great Plains Botanical Society
P.O. Box 461
Hot Springs, SD 57747

Green Spring Gardens Park
4603 Green Spring Rd.
Alexandria, VA 22312

Greenwell Ethnobotanical Garden
P.O. Box 1053
Captain Cook, HI 96704

Hayes Regional Arboretum
801 Elks Rd.
Richmond, IN 47374

Idaho Botanical Garden
2355 Old Penitentiary Rd.
Boise, ID 83712

Inniswood Metro Gardens
940 Hempstead Rd.
Westerville, OH 43081

Jungle Gardens
General Delivery
Avery Island, LA 70513

Lakewold Gardens
P.O. Box 98092
Tacoma, WA 98498

Londontown Public House &
Gardens
839 Londontown Rd.
Edgewater, MD 21222

Wilbur D. May Arboretum and
Botanical Garden
1502 Washington St.
Reno, NV 89503

Medford Leas
Route 70
Medford, NJ 08055

Missouri Botanical Garden
P.O. Box 299
St. Louis, MO 63166

Morton Arboretum
Route 53
Lisle, IL 60532

Mt. Cuba Center
P.O. Box 3570
Greenville, DE 19807-0570

Myriad Botanical Gardens
100 Myriad Gardens
Oklahoma City, OK 73102

Paul Bunyan Conservation
Arboretum
P.O. Box 375
Brainerd, MN 56401

Pine Tree State Arboretum
P.O. Box 344
Augusta, ME 04330

Red Butte Garden and Arboretum
University of Utah
390 Wakara Way
Salt Lake City, UT 84108

Sol y Sombra
4018 Old Santa Fe Trail
Santa Fe, NM 87505

University of Montana
Facilities Services Dept.
Campus Dr.
Missoula, MT 59812-1381

Vail Alpine Garden Foundation
183 Gore Creek Dr.
Vail, CO 81657

National Park Service Regional Offices

Alaska Region
National Park Service
2525 Gambell St.
Anchorage, AK 99503

Pacific Northwest Region
National Park Service
83 South King St., #212
Seattle, WA 98104

Western Region
National Park Service
600 Harrison St. #600
San Francisco, CA 94107

Rocky Mountain Region
National Park Service
P.O. Box 25287
Denver, CO 80225

Southwest Region
National Park Service
P.O. Box 728
Santa Fe, NM 87501

Midwest Region
National Park Service
1709 Jackson St.
Omaha, NE 68102

Southeast Region
National Park Service
Richard B. Russell Federal Bldg.
75 Spring St., S.W.
Atlanta, GA 30303

Mid-Atlantic Region
National Park Service
143 South Third St.
Philadelphia, PA 19106

National Capital Region
National Park Service
1100 Ohio Dr., S.W.
Washington, D.C. 20242

North Atlantic Region
National Park Service
15 State St.
Boston, MA 02109

VGM CAREER BOOKS

CAREER DIRECTORIES
Careers Encyclopedia
Dictionary of Occupational
Titles
Occupational Outlook
Handbook

CAREERS FOR
Animal Lovers
Bookworms
Computer Buffs
Crafty People
Culture Lovers
Environmental Types
Film Buffs
Foreign Language Aficionados
Good Samaritans
Gourmets
History Buffs
Kids at Heart
Nature Lovers
Night Owls
Number Crunchers
Plant Lovers
Shutterbugs
Sports Nuts
Travel Buffs

CAREERS IN
Accounting; Advertising;
Business; Child Care;
Communications; Computers;
Education; Engineering;
the Environment; Finance;
Government; Health Care;
High Tech; Journalism; Law;
Marketing; Medicine;
Science; Social &
Rehabilitation Services

CAREER PLANNING
Admissions Guide to Selective
Business Schools
Beating Job Burnout
Beginning Entrepreneur
Career Planning &
Development for College
Students & Recent Graduates
Career Change

Careers Checklists
Cover Letters They Don't
Forget
Executive Job Search Strategies
Guide to Basic Cover Letter
Writing
Guide to Basic Resume Writing
Guide to Temporary
Employment
Job Interviews Made Easy
Joyce Lain Kennedy's Career
Book
Out of Uniform
Resumes Made Easy
Slam Dunk Resumes
Successful Interviewing for
College Seniors
Time for a Change

CAREER PORTRAITS
Animals   Nursing
Cars   Sports
Computers   Teaching
Music   Travel

GREAT JOBS FOR
Communications Majors
English Majors
Foreign Language Majors
History Majors
Psychology Majors

HOW TO
Approach an Advertising
Agency and Walk Away with
the Job You Want
Bounce Back Quickly After
Losing Your Job
Choose the Right Career
Find Your New Career Upon
Retirement
Get & Keep Your First Job
Get Hired Today
Get into the Right Business
School
Get into the Right Law School
Get People to Do Things Your
Way
Have a Winning Job Interview

Hit the Ground Running in
Your New Job
Improve Your Study Skills
Jump Start a Stalled Career
Land a Better Job
Launch Your Career in TV
News
Make the Right Career Moves
Market Your College Degree
Move from College into a
Secure Job
Negotiate the Raise You
Deserve
Prepare a Curriculum Vitae
Prepare for College
Run Your Own Home Business
Succeed in College
Succeed in High School
Write a Winning Resume
Write Successful Cover Letters
Write Term Papers & Reports
Write Your College Application
Essay

OPPORTUNITIES IN
This extensive series provides
detailed information on nearly
150 individual career fields.

RESUMES FOR
Advertising Careers
Banking and Financial Careers
Business Management Careers
College Students &
Recent Graduates
Communications Careers
Education Careers
Engineering Careers
Environmental Careers
50 + Job Hunters
Health and Medical Careers
High School Graduates
High Tech Careers
Law Careers
Midcareer Job Changes
Sales and Marketing Careers
Scientific and Technical Careers
Social Service Careers
The First-Time Job Hunter

 **VGM Career Horizons**
a division of NTC Publishing Group
4255 West Touhy Avenue
Lincolnwood, Illinois 60646–1975